Appla

Dare to D

We all face overwhelming experiences—times when we can't see the way out. Cathy has walked that road and graciously shares her insights from the journey. By pointing her readers first to Scripture, then to action steps and prayer, she leads them to the light and the way to wholeness again.

Lorraine Myrholm
Author and Speaker

Encouragement, reassurance and hope are on every page of this insightful devotional book. Cathy shares stories, experiences, and Scripture to challenge us to walk boldly along the path of life, embracing the loving presence and care of God, and to discover "life in all its fullness."

Margaret Roller
International Conference and Seminar Speaker

Cathy Mogus knows how to guide us through life's valleys in a practical and biblical way. In *Dare to Dance Again,* she tells real life stories to gently provide us with steps of practical application, solid biblical truths from the book of Psalms, and heartfelt prayers to pray as you travel down life's difficult paths. This is a must-have resource for anyone who is struggling or knows of someone who is struggling through life's valleys. Thank you, Cathy, for your wisdom and openness to share.

Janet Boivin
Director of Women's Ministry
South Delta Baptist Church (Delta, B.C.)

Cathy blends her uplifting stories with the inspiring joys of the Psalms and gives us new ways of making difficult decisions to meet the stresses and challenges of our everyday lives. Her wonderful collage of vignettes is not only an affirmation only of God's grace, but will serve in a powerful way to illustrate that faith, hope, and love are the guides that can bring us peace.

Dr. Edison Bardock
Alberta Northwest Conference, United Church of Canada

In this book Cathy holds your hand and walks beside you as she shares your moments of trial, sadness, or confusion. Since she rests in Jesus, she is able to talk to you about Him. An engaging book filled with beautiful prayers. Her candor is remarkable.

Julianne Huang
Roman Catholic Catechism Instructor

This book draws me into the presence of the Lord with each story and related Bible verses. Cathy uniquely draws from life events and circumstances. She brings me to face life issues creatively with God's help by asking me to take "Two Steps Back," which brings my focus to how God is working in my life. In "Two Steps Forward" she encourages me with God's Word to make positive steps of faith. Then with "One Step More" she adds a confirming prayer. This book will be by my Bible and journal for many refreshing times to come.

Carma Carlson-Bergen
Stillwood Camp and Conference Centre, staff member
(Lindell Beach, B.C.)

Dare to Dance Again

Dare to Dance Again

In Step With God When Life Trips You Up

Cathy Mogus

Golden Circle Press, Vancouver, BC, Canada

www.goldencirclepress.com

© Copyright 2011, 2017 by Cathaleen Mogus.

Originally published under the title *Dare to Dance Again: Steps from the Psalms When Life Trips You Up.*

All rights reserved.

Unless otherwise indicated, all Scripture quotations are taken from THE HOLY BIBLE, NEW INTERNATIONAL VERSION. Copyright © 1973, 1978, 1984, 2011 by International Bible Society. All rights reserved.

Verses marked TLB are taken from the The Living Bible. Copyright © 1971 by Tyndale House Publishers. All rights reserved.

Verses marked NKJV are taken from the New King James Version. Copyright © 1982 by Thomas Nelson, Inc. All rights reserved.

Verses marked KJV are taken from the King James Version of the Bible.

Verses from the *Good News Bible* © 1994 by the Bible Societies/HarperCollins Publishers Ltd. UK, *Good News Bible* © American Bible Society 1966, 1971, 1976, 1992. All rights reserved.

Verses marked NLT are taken from the New Living Translation, copyright © 1996, 2004, 2015. Used by permission of Tyndale House Publishers, Inc. All rights reserved.

Scripture taken from *The Message*. Copyright © 1993, 1994, 1995, 1996, 2000, 2001, 2002. Used by permission of NavPress Publishing Group. All rights reserved.

Cover Image by Nerify/Shutterstock.com

ISBN-13: 978-0995251045 (sc)
ISBN-13: 978-0995251038 (e)

To my children,

for whom

I kept—and keep—dancing.

Thanks for Stepping Up!

~ Writing this book was a long and tedious journey with many starts and stops (some long ones!) along the way. It was often easier to write magazine articles than to keep focused on "the book." And now that the race has been run, I have numerous people to thank for encouraging me to cross the finish line.

~ When Allen married me in 1994, he had no idea what he was getting into! Not only did I rob him of his office and desk, I hushed him up and hustled him out so I could write. He'll tell you it hasn't always been easy. But this book would never have been written without his support and patience.

~ I have my children, Andrew, Travis, and Shanda, to thank for buying me my first computer for my fiftieth birthday. In those days, they had little cash but lots of love. They each contributed a piece (hard drive, monitor, keyboard, and printer). It sure beat my old electric typewriter!

~ Each one of them was in my heart and mind when I commenced writing *Dare to Dance Again.* I wanted to record for them the proof that God can utilize the most painful experiences in life to make us stronger and more useful to Him. Life hasn't always been easy for them either. I am so proud of their resilience, their determination. They have inspired me to keep writing, to keep praying, and to keep dancing.

~ I want to thank my parents, Paul and Virginia Cruger, who are in heaven now, for giving me my writing genes. And who knows what I would have penned if it had not been for the spiritual legacy that they gave me?

~ I deeply appreciate my sister Carolyn Williams, who has been a constant source of strength and encouragement in my battles with life and writing. We have cried and prayed together more times than I care to count. Her walk with God has influenced her little sister more than she'll ever know.

~ I am so very grateful for all those who took the time and effort to read the manuscript and offer editorial and content suggestions. I especially want to thank Edison Bardock, Julianne Huang, and Lois Bouchard for their edits in the first stages of the manuscript. I also want to thank Christina Newberry for taking on the final edit in such a professional and quick manner. And I appreciate my son Travis Karr's help with this revision.

~ I must thank my friends Patti Garneau, Karen Beitel, Margaret de Cassseres Wilson, Kay Smith, Edna Janzen, and Lynn VanHerwaarden for their encouragement and prayer support.

~ And last of all, I want to thank Janet Boivin for living close enough to God to nudge me (shove might be a better word) into actually publishing *Dare to Dance Again*. I have no idea what would have happened to this book if she had not shown up for lunch at Tim Horton's—and insisted I complete the job.

Before You Begin...

If life is treating you well right now, if you're in a good space, this book is probably not for you. Honestly. But if you're wading through the deep waters of a heartache or crisis—or know of someone who is—then bingo!

The meditations in this book are based on verses from the Psalms. When I was experiencing difficult times, this portion of God's Word helped me the most. The middle section of my little blue Bible is well underlined and highlighted! Dates are written in the margins. There are even tearstains.

David, the composer of many of those ancient songs, was an expert on suffering. As Israel's king, he led a colorful life marked by intense pain. He was hated—and hunted—by his boss. He was belittled by his wife. He had an affair. His body was racked by disease. He had enemies everywhere. He lost a child. He even murdered a man. And yet he kept writing songs that reflected triumph over tragedy, faith over failure.

Each devotional is followed by *Two Steps Back, Two Steps Forward,* and *One Step More.* *Two Steps Back* gives the reader two specific things to think about in connection with the devotional. *Two Steps Forward* suggests two things the reader can do to help move forward toward wholeness. *One Step More* is a prayer that can be read in silence or aloud. This may be helpful to those who are new to prayer—or to articulating needs and feelings.

Someone who has overcome heartache by God's grace and help doesn't need permission to dance! Take David. The Bible says he was "dancing before the Lord with all his might" (2 Sam. 6:14) after the Ark of the Covenant was finally brought back to Jerusalem. To Israel's king, bringing home "the presence of

God" from enemy territory was major. And not only did he dance, he danced *daringly*.

As an act of worship, he removed his royal robes and put on a simple linen garb worn by priests. And then he danced like crazy. He later told his not-so-amused wife, "I am willing to act like a fool in order to show my joy in the Lord" (2 Sam. 6:21, TLB).

Do you long for hope and joy and peace? Do you yearn for answers and guidance? Do you want to someday dance before God in gratefulness for answered prayers? Well, I suggest you keep reading this book, try the backward and forward steps—and keep praying. God hasn't brought you this far for nothing. He wants you to dance again *for Him*.

Called Higher

You turned my wailing into dancing;
you removed my sackcloth and clothed me with joy,
that my heart may sing your praises and
not be silent. Lord my God, I will praise you forever.

Psalm 30:11, 12

We met at the orientation session of a Christian writers' conference. Kathi had auburn hair, a wide smile, and sparkling blue eyes. I liked her immediately. I was disappointed we wouldn't be in classes together. "I'll probably never see you again," I said before we parted, "but it really was nice meeting you."

But we kept running into each other. In a hallway, on a sidewalk, in a lunch line. There was no other one person I connected with more during those five days than Kathi. We kept smiling and waving at one another. "I can't believe it's you *again*," I'd say—or she'd say.

Heavy rain was pelting the conference grounds like some evil target when it happened again. I'd lost my umbrella and Kathi invited me to huddle under hers. We both agreed there must be a reason—maybe a divine reason—why we kept bumping into each other. "Tell me about yourself," I told her, playing the role of a reporter.

Kathi said she was a stay-at-home wife and mom of three teenage boys. She didn't consider herself a writer, but she and a friend were putting together a women's Bible study. I then told her I was an empty nester and had been writing magazine articles for some time. I told her about my almost-completed book.

1

"What's it about?" she asked.

"It's a devotional for those going through a crisis."

"It sounds like the kind of book I could have used when my daughter died," Kathi almost whispered. Tears filled my eyes as she then shared what it was like to lose a three-year-old to illness. The grief, the questions, the almost-destroyed marriage.

"I wanted someone to call me higher," Kathi concluded. "I wanted to be challenged in my faith."

I gave her a copy of my book proposal and we went our separate ways. Later that day, I glanced up to see her on an overhead walkway. She leaned over the handrail and waved it at me.

"The first Bible verse I read in your book was the first scripture God gave me after my daughter died!" she almost shouted. "Don't give up!"

I wanted someone to call me higher... It seemed a bit odd that someone would want to be spiritually motivated when they had just lost a child. It would be much easier to give in to despair, depression—and anger. But Kathi had obviously experienced enough of God in her life to know that it was possible for Him to turn her "wailing into dancing." And she knew she would need plenty of extra help to get there.

I wanted to be challenged in my faith. At the heart of the Christian faith is the belief that "all things God works for the good of those who love Him, who have been called according to His purpose" (Romans 8:28). *All things.* Even the death of a child. Somehow He takes our deepest pain and uses it to strengthen our relationship with Him and to achieve His purpose for our time here on earth. He never "wastes our sorrows"—if we partner with Him in the dance of life.

I hope that as you continue to read this book, you will feel a sense of being called higher. And that through all the pain and confusion of the moment, you will come to understand that you are being prepared for something grand, something far beyond your hopes and expectations.

Two Steps Back

- How to you feel about the idea of being "called higher?"
- Do you think anything good can come out of your present painful situation?

Two Steps Forward

- Write out the emotions you are feeling right now (anger, fear, rejection, etc.).
- Read Psalm 23.

One Step More

Dear God, You know that this journey is one that I never wanted or asked for. Please give me the support I will need and the strength to carry on. And help me to someday understand that You can use even this for a higher purpose. Amen.

The Promise

Yes, my soul, find rest in God;
my hope comes from him.

Psalm 62:5

I remember the exact spot in the church aisle where Roy stopped me. Our eyes locked. "Cathy, the sun *will* shine again," he whispered, touching my arm. That's all he said, and he walked away. My eyes filled with tears.

The sun will shine again. If anyone knew what those words meant, Roy did. He was a well-known and well-liked man in our small community. When he lost his job through unfavorable circumstances, the news hit our local paper. He and his wife were then forced to sell their beautiful newly built home. I ached for them.

But little by little, they rebuilt their lives. Their family, friends, and church supported them through the dark days. One prayer after another was answered. The sun began to beam down on Roy and his family once more.

My problem was of a different sort. At that point I was still reeling from the agony of an unwanted divorce. After almost twenty years of what I thought was a good marriage, my husband told me he was leaving. The pain was excruciating. As my self-esteem hit rock bottom, I was convinced I would never dance in the sunshine again.

Roy's five-word "prophecy" in the church aisle that day clicked something within me. It gave me hope—and determination. Somehow I knew that if I was ever going to crawl out of my dark pit of despair, I would have to change my way of thinking.

If Roy was right—and I prayed he was—my life would one day return to some sort of normalcy. Spring *would* come. The sun *would* shine again. I instinctively knew I would have to cling to that hope in the tough days ahead.

One of the first Bible verses God led me to was Psalm 30:5. It was His promise to me that someday I would stop crying; someday the wounds would heal. That when the horrible night was finally over, I would dance for joy at the breaking of a new day.

You, too, can claim this promise. Only God knows what is ahead for you, but if you take one step toward Him, there is hope—great hope.

Two Steps Back

- What is keeping you from having joy in your life?
- Are you willing to let God give you His peace in your pain?

Two Steps Forward

- Read Psalm 30.
- Call a friend.

One Step More

Dear God, when my darkness seems to span an eternity, please help me to remember You are the Creator of every new dawn. Thank You for Your promise that my weeping will last only for this night—and that joy is coming. Amen.

The Incomplete Story

We went through fire and water,
but you brought us to a place of abundance.

Psalm 66:12

"They should have let him die instead of making him go through all that," our houseguest commented while reading the morning paper.

I knew the article to which he was referring. It was the story of a forty-ton tractor-trailer losing its brakes as it approached a tollbooth. As it crashed into the last vehicle in line, the impact ruptured the gas tank of a car holding two men and a twenty-two-month-old baby. The men, the child's father and uncle, each thought the other had the toddler. The child was still strapped in his car seat when the vehicle burst into a ball of flames.

A stranger reached in and pulled the child to safety. Protected only by a diaper, the baby was burned over eighty-five per cent of his body. He lost his ears, his left hand, the fingers on his right hand, and the flesh and skin covering part of his skull. There was little structure left to his face.

This was as far as our visitor had read.

"That's not the end of the story," I told him. "Read the rest."

The child underwent surgery more than forty times in four years. Now an adult, he describes his childhood as a time spent growing up in a hospital and looking like a little monster.

He was encouraged, however, by his parents and his Christian faith to think positively. Instead of giving up or becoming bitter, he made the best of what he had left. He excelled at school and sports and became an accomplished speaker. He was class president in university. He is now helping others face their own tragedies.

None of us know what the end of our story is going to be. But we can use our faith in God and what we have left in life to bring about positive results. Remember: "For I know the plans I have for you," declares the LORD, "plans to prosper you and not to harm you, plans to give you hope and a future" (Jeremiah 29:11).

Don't give up now. This is not the end of your story.[1]

Two Steps Back

- What discourages you the most today?
- Who can you contact for a spiritual boost?

Two Steps Forward

- Write out Jeremiah 29:11. Place it where you can read it daily.
- Make contact with a Christian mentor.

One Step More

Sometimes, God, I feel like giving up. Thank You for reminding me that You see the end from the beginning. Give me the grace I need to allow You to give this story the ending You've already planned. Amen.

A Tap on the Shoulder

When I awake, I am still with you.

Psalm 139:18

An eighteen-year-old boy fell over a ledge while descending a snowfield on Washington's Mt. Baker. His climbing partners attempted to rescue him, but with freezing hands he couldn't grip the rope they offered. While they went for help, he curled his body into the fetal position to keep warm. As time passed, however, death seemed certain.

Sometime later, much to his surprise, the teenager felt a hand touch him. His friends had found three firefighters who were preparing for a climb and told them of the boy's plight. Using ropes, pulleys, and harnesses, one of them dropped down the crevice to begin the rescue.

"In his mind, the final moment was at hand," the county sheriff later told a reporter. "In his deepest moment of despair, there was a tap on his shoulder."

This may be a moment in your life when you need a nudge to assure you your heartache will not last forever. A tap on your shoulder. A spark of hope in your darkness.

Whatever you do, don't give up. You don't know when that moment will come. Just like the boys who found the needed help for their friend, so the prayers of others have reached the throne of God for you. You can be assured that help is on the way.

Our timing of things is not always synchronized with God's timing. We want help NOW—ASAP—but He often waits in order to give us the best help possible. If those boys had tried the rescue themselves, their friend probably would have died. The wait—no matter how horrible—was the best thing in the end. So hang in there. It won't be long before you'll feel a tap on *your* shoulder.

Two Steps Back

- Who do you think might be praying for you on a regular basis?
- Do you believe God will answer their prayers?

Two Steps Forward

- Read Psalm 145:14–21.
- Listen to gospel music that will soothe your spirit and encourage you to wait for God's perfect solutions.

One Step More

Dear God, thank You that You are still with me even when I cannot see Your plan. Please give me the patience to wait—and the courage to respond to Your tap on my shoulder. Amen.

Eggshells

*I stay close to you; your right
hand upholds me.*

Psalm 63:8

As I took my morning walk today, I spotted a tiny eggshell on the side of the path. I picked it up and gently examined it. The broken speckled teal shell resembled a wee bowl.

As I continued walking at a brisk pace, I closed my fingers around my fragile treasure so as not to crush it. I could feel it bouncing on the soft cushion of my palm.

I thought how we sometimes resemble that little shell. God has created every one of us as a thing of beauty, and yet we are so fragile. We get hurt and cracked. And when He sees our brokenness on the path of life, He gently picks us up and holds us tenderly in the palm of His hand.

He knows that if He holds us too tight, we will soon be crushed. So, in His love and wisdom, He allows us space—room to bounce around. From our perspective, we think we are going to be flattened by all the movement, by all the changes. From *His* perspective, there is no way He is going to drop us. As long as we are in the palm of His hand, we are perfectly safe.

That little shell had to be broken for the miracle of new life to take place. So we must endure hardships for our lives to be productive. But in the process, God picks us up.

Have you noticed that as we bounce around, He keeps walking and taking us with Him? Someday our heartaches will cease, and He will set us down just where He wants us.

I placed that little shell on my desk to remind me of God's loving care. As the prophet Isaiah said so long ago, "Can a mother forget the baby at her breast and have no compassion on the child she has borne? Though she may forget, I will not forget you! See, I have engraved you on the palms of my hands; your walls are ever before me" (Isaiah 49:15–16).

Two Steps Back

- What is your biggest fear today?
- Are you willing to give that fear to God?

Two Steps Forward

- Read Psalm 62:5–8.
- Say a prayer starting with these words: "Dear God, You know that I am afraid of…" Then end with the following prayer.

One Step More

Thank You for keeping me safe in the palms of Your hands. Remind me that no matter how hard I am bounced around, You will never let go of me—and that You have a destination in mind for me. Amen.

Prayer Journal

I love the LORD, for he heard
my voice;
he heard my cry for mercy.

Psalm 116:1

A few years back I bought my first prayer journal. On the inside cover of the little booklet there was space for one's name, the date, and this verse from the Bible: "Call to Me, and I will answer you, and show you great and mighty things, which you do not know" (Jeremiah 33:3, NKJ).

There was space for requests for personal needs, family concerns, friends, church, the nation, and various ministries. At the end of the booklet was a place to record answers to prayer and the dates on which they occurred. I found it to be a great prayer tool.

Keeping a prayer journal can be especially helpful when you are searching for answers during a difficult period. First of all, it can keep you praying. Secondly, it gives you an agenda to follow when your mind wants to wander. And it forces you to talk to God honestly and openly. Journaling your prayers is a tangible way to view your spiritual progress, to see how your requests have been answered. It serves as a faith builder. I noted, for instance, a prayer request for a Christian friend who was dating an unbeliever. A year later, almost to the date, I penned in the answer: "Shelley called to say she wants to leave Joe. 'It's Joe or Jesus!'" I couldn't help but write PTL (Praise the Lord) next to that notation.

Prayer journals can also be used to watch the progress of a particular request. Sometimes I like to leave extra space for certain requests.

If your prayer time is a struggle, why not try a personal prayer journal? All it takes is a small notebook. Make columns for dates and particulars of prayer requests and answers. And remember, an answer can be yes, no, or wait. This may be just the thing to help you see the big picture—the way God sees it.

Two Steps Back

- Have you ever kept track of your prayers by writing them down?
- Do you think this would build your faith—or discourage you?

Two Steps Forward

- Read Luke 18:1–8.
- Purchase a prayer journal from your local Christian bookstore or use a notebook to start journaling your prayers.

One Step More

Dear God, thank You for practical ways You have provided for us to grow in You. Help me to use what works best for me. Amen.

Tsunami

You rule over the surging sea;
when its waves mount up, you still them.

Psalm 89:9

Good Friday,1964, 10:30 p.m. Andy and Mary Cruckshank's seventeen-year-old son, Rick, was in bed listening to the radio when he heard the news that a large earthquake had shaken Alaska, and a tidal wave was expected to hit the shores of Canada's west coast.

The Cruckshanks lived in a small logging camp on Amai Inlet, nine miles from the Pacific Ocean. Although they were right on the beach, the news didn't alarm them as they felt they were too far from Alaska to be concerned.

When Mary heard what sounded like a downpour of heavy hail, she became alarmed. It was a clear night. She quickly looked out the window. Waves were bubbling and rolling in with terrific force. She yelled to Rick to warn others in the camp while she and Andy woke up the younger children.

The water was rising fast. All went dark as it covered the generator plant, their only source of electricity. Pandemonium broke loose as the bunkhouse and cookhouse disappeared. When Mary opened her back door and realized the water was still rising, she cried out to God in desperation: "Lord, make the water go down!" The water level dropped immediately. It gave everyone time enough to run for higher ground.

Where did Mary get her faith to ask God to make the water subside? I believe it came from her personal relationship with Him and from experience.

Mary first became acquainted with God as a child during the "hungry thirties." Her entire family accepted Jesus Christ at a tent meeting. She observed how her parents trusted Him from then on for their daily food and other needs.

After marrying Andy, Mary learned much about faith while raising her little family in isolated logging camps. She prayed her way through storms, rough boat trips, turbulent plane rides, and forest fires. By the time the tsunami occurred, she had no trouble believing God could control a tidal wave.

Someone once said, "A lot of little prayers as we go through life would save a lot of long ones in case of emergencies." Answered prayers boost your faith in God's love and power.

Look at your trials as tools God can use to help you practice trusting Him. Someday, when the waves in your life rise higher than they've ever been, you will know without a doubt that He does rule the raging of *all* your seas.

Two Steps Back

- How has God answered your prayers in the past?
- Have your answered prayers helped you to have faith in more difficult circumstances?

Two Steps Forward

- Read Psalm 77:10–15.
- Write in your journal some of the ways God has helped you in a similar situation. For instance, if you are ill, have you ever experienced Christ's healing touch?

One Step More

Dear God, help me never to forget that You can calm any storm—even mine. Give me the courage to face my problems. May the lessons I learn be used for Your glory. Amen.

Faith, Hope, and Love

I am overwhelmed and desperate,
and you alone know
which way I ought to turn...

Psalm 142:3 (TLB)

A number of years ago I was fired from a job I desperately needed. I'd worked in a six-doctor medical clinic for more than two years. It was the ideal job for a single parent. Good pay, great hours, and solid friendships formed over many cups of coffee.

I felt humiliated and betrayed—and terrified. I couldn't shake my fears. What now? How would I support my teenagers or even pay the rent? Who would hire me? How was I to face anyone?

When I shared my frustrations with a friend, she offered to pray with me. I have no idea what she prayed, but evidently God was listening. During the next few weeks, He miraculously calmed my fears.

He did it through three things the apostle Paul said remain when our security blankets are pulled out from beneath us—faith, hope, and love.

I discovered faith is like a snowplow. When I used it to push away my doubts, it opened up a path of possibilities before me. Believing in myself was the first step. I tried honestly to assess why I had been fired, but it was difficult to analyze my errors when I didn't know what they were. I did know that the clinic was in a financial crisis.

Although my work had appealed to my love for organizing, it did not encourage my creative side. I had done some freelance writing and speaking. Was this God's way of nudging me into something more fulfilling? I decided to trust God with this one.

Eventually I landed a job selling ads for a magazine. This gave me the courage to apply for another sales position, where I became a manager within a short time. That job took me to a convention where I met Allen, now my husband. And that led me to where I am now—a happy homemaker who has the time and resources to write and speak again!

Faith in God and yourself will plow a path of hope before you. You may be treated unfairly, but His love for you will help you win in the end.[2]

Two Steps Back

- Have you had the experience of one thing leading to another?
- Did seeing the big picture give you hope?

Two Steps Forward

- Read Psalm 143.
- Make a list in your journal of the positive things that have happened to you this past week.

One Step More

Dear God, whenever I feel overwhelmed, please give me enough faith to keep my hopes alive. May Your love for me keep me from despair. Amen.

Passing Storms

I remain confident of this:
I will see the goodness of the LORD
in the land of the living.

Psalm 27:13

Allen and I once spent five weeks in Whistler, B.C., Canada's world-renowned ski resort. Allen installed air conditioning and heating in multi-million-dollar homes while I wrote the outline for this book in a condo provided by his company.

We were blessed by a few gorgeous days, but then dark clouds rolled in over the mountains. One morning, as I was driving from the ski village to the condo, sheets of lightening flashed across the sky above me. Thunder shook the truck. Without warning, I was suddenly driving in the worst rainstorm I'd encountered since our El Niño spring.

But the big surprise came when I sat at my desk an hour later. My view out the window showed a blue sky with a few fluffy white clouds. Even the pavement in the parking lot below was partially dry. Where had the monster storm gone?

I thought about the troubles we encounter in life. They take us by surprise, and we have no idea how long they will last at the time. Sometimes by the size of them we can't imagine the sun beaming down any too soon.

When we returned home to pick up supplies for Allen's job, a personal storm broke. Severe chest pains knocked him to the bathroom floor one morning while he was shaving. I rushed him to the hospital, praying all the way. An angiogram was ordered, but to our dismay, he was put on a three-month waiting list!

Allen took a leave of absence from his job. The long wait caused more anxiety—and chest pains. We constantly reminded ourselves that God was in control, not a faulty medical system.

Thankfully, a cardiologist agreed to perform the angiogram ahead of schedule. We were baffled—but greatly relieved—when Allen was told he had a perfect heart!

Turbulence in weather and life does not last forever. Every storm must weaken and disappear sooner or later. And every heartbreak has the possibility to heal at some point. A few clouds may linger, but you will survive.

Two Steps Back

- What has been your worst storm so far, not counting this one?
- How was it weakened? Have any "clouds" lingered?

Two Steps Forward

- Read Psalm 18:28–36.
- Thank God for how He has helped you in the past. Be specific!

One Step More

Thank you, Lord, that this storm will not last forever. I know someday You will push back these clouds with Your wind of love—and I will see the sun once more. Thank you! Amen.

Fighting Smart

He sends his command to the earth;
his word runs swiftly.

Psalm 147:15

In 606 B.C., Daniel, a member of Israel's nobility, became a captive when Babylon besieged Jerusalem. Nebuchadnezzar, Babylon's king, placed Daniel and other promising young Israelite men in positions of authority after a three-year training period.

Although he learned the Babylonian language and literature, Daniel never forgot his country, nor his God. When he received a revelation from God regarding a great war to come, he fasted and prayed for three weeks.

One day while standing on the bank of the Tigris River, Daniel saw a man who had a face "like lightening" and a voice "like the sound of a multitude." He immediately fell to the ground trembling. What followed was an incredible vision. He was told that God had responded to his prayers by sending out a command:

"Don't be frightened, Daniel, for your request has been heard in heaven and was answered the very first day you began to fast before the Lord and pray for understanding; that very day I was sent here to meet you. But for twenty-one days the mighty Evil Spirit who overrules the kingdom of Persia blocked my way. Then Michael, one of the top officers of the heavenly army, came to help me, so that I was able to break through these spirit rulers of Persia. Now I am here to tell you what will happen" (Daniel 10:12–14, TLB).

I wonder how many answers to our prayers have been delayed because of spiritual warfare! We don't have to be frightened, however, by this possibility. The apostle Paul gives us the solution: *"So use every piece of God's armor to resist the enemy whenever he attacks, and when it is all over, you will be standing up"* (Eph. 6:13, TLB).

What is God's armor? First of all, a personal relationship with Jesus Christ. Then, as you pray and read His Word, you will receive the truth and peace that comes from following His directions. God sends out commands in response to your prayers, but you need to position yourself to receive them.

Two Steps Back

- Do you feel you are in spiritual warfare?
- What sort of "armor" have you put on to protect yourself?

Two Steps Forward

- Read Ephesians 6:10–20.
- List the pieces of the "armor of God" mentioned in these verses. Under each item, write down how this can apply to you today.

One Step More

Lord, thank You for reminding me that Satan does not want me to win this battle. I know I cannot fight it alone, so I trust You to send the help I need. Thank You for the angels who are listening to Your commands concerning me. Amen.

His Delight

"The LORD be exalted,
who delights in the well-being of his servant."

Psalm 35:27

My sons, Andrew and Travis, were on wrestling teams in high school. I tried to make it to as many matches as possible and cheered my heart out. I thoroughly enjoyed watching them and was elated whenever one of them won a match. When Travis won a gold medal in a divisional tournament, I was thrilled and couldn't wait to share the good news with my friends.

But watching them wrestle was not always easy. If I knew they were in pain, my maternal instincts took over. I wanted to yell, "Stop!" to their opponents, but I closed my eyes—and mouth—instead. I knew that it took great effort and discomfort for them to become winners.

My sons are now in their prime adult years. I like to believe I am still their biggest fan. There's nothing I enjoy better than watching them enjoy life and succeed in their careers. But still I sometimes have to close my eyes (usually in prayer!)—and my mouth—whenever I know they are struggling.

In the same way, your Heavenly Father is cheering you on. Our verse today says He "delights in the well-being of his servant." The New Living Bible paraphrases it to read, "Great is the Lord who enjoys helping his child!" It brings Him great pleasure to make you happy. He loves to see you smile!

So why does He seem distant at times? Why doesn't He answer your gut-wrenching prayers immediately? Where was He when all this happened to you?

He was still in the cheerleading section. But He knows you must experience some pain (maybe a great deal!) in order to be a success for Him. And when the battle has been won, you will hear His applause above all others. Believe me, His "well done" will be worth it all!

Two Steps Back

- Who are the cheerleaders in your life?
- Why do they want you to succeed?

Two Steps Forward

- Read Jeremiah 29:11–13.
- List the times you know God has been cheering you on to victory.

One Step More

Thank you, Father, for your great love for me. Help me never to forget that You are on my side. Help me hear Your applause above my struggle and value it more than anything. Amen.

Stand Tall!

The LORD lifts up those who are bowed down,
the LORD loves the righteous.

Psalm 146:8

Jesus was teaching in a synagogue one Sabbath when He noticed a woman severely bent over. He called her over and touched her. She instantly stood straight, something she had not done in eighteen years. She was so excited that all she could do was praise God.

The leader of the synagogue was not impressed. He accused Jesus of working on the Sabbath and shouted instructions to the crowd to come for healing on other days.

In His reply, Jesus pointed out the fact that the Sabbath was the appropriate day for healing someone "Satan has kept bound for eighteen long years" (Luke 13:16).

Satan will keep you "bowed down" in any way he can—and for as long as he can. His mandate is to shatter your self-esteem and faith in God to the max.

Jesus, on the other hand, wants to free you. He acknowledges these have been "long years" (or weeks and months). He knows how you yearn to speed up the healing process.

It's interesting to note that Jesus called the woman over to him—and her response was essential to her healing. "Draw near to God and He will draw near to you" (James 4:8). As you position yourself for His help (the woman still attended church in spite of her pain and pride), He will touch you.

Have you noticed that low self-esteem and poor posture often go together? God wants to free you to stand tall, to be confident in yourself and in Him. You can put your shoulders back and face whatever is ahead of you through His power and grace.

Two Steps Back

- Do you believe that Satan is real?
- Have you been aware of his activities in your life? In your present situation?

Two Steps Forward

- Read 1 Peter 5:6–11.
- Resist Satan's power by praying, reading the Bible, and keeping in fellowship with other Christians on a daily basis.

One Step More

Dear Lord, I give You the burden I am carrying today. I acknowledge that it has weighed me down in spirit and body. Please touch me—and help me to stand tall for You. Amen.

Feelings

You know when I sit and when I rise;
you perceive my thoughts from afar.

Psalm 139:2

Do not feel guilty about *how you feel* about what is happening right now. Feelings are neither good nor bad. How you feel is how you feel. Period.

You may be experiencing depression, anger, guilt, worry. It's okay. If you didn't feel anything during a time like this, you wouldn't be normal.

You have reasons for feeling the way you do. After his wife's death, C.S. Lewis wrote, "You can't see anything properly while your eyes are blurred with tears."[3] In other words, don't be so hard on yourself, especially during the first stages of grief.

Don't be too concerned about others understanding precisely what you are experiencing. The Bible says, "Only the person involved can know his own bitterness or joy—no one else can really share it" (Proverbs 14:10, TLB).

The good news is that God alone knows how you feel—and He understands. Isaiah prophesied that Jesus would be "acquainted with grief." He knows what it is like to be hated, rejected, punished unjustly, and persecuted.[4]

For more than fifty years, Amy Carmichael (1895–1951) ministered to the needy children of South India. She knew what suffering was all about. Her thought was that the feelings pass. She wrote: *"Let us press on through all feelings of sloth or discouragement or fear, to the place where our God can speak to us in the stillness, and hold us close to His heart."*[5]

As you tell God how your sorrow is affecting you, allow Him to comfort you. You will eventually be able to "press on through all feelings"—and see the ways He has chosen to help you.

Two Steps Back

- What is the dominant feeling you are experiencing today? Anger, fear, peace, resentment, jealousy?
- Are you experiencing guilt for feeling this way?

Two Steps Forward

- Read Psalm 142.
- Write in your journal how you are *feeling* today.

One Step More

Dear God, You know exactly how I am feeling right now. Thank You for sending Your Son who has forgiven my sins— and identified with my pain. Help me to accept Your love and help. Amen.

Tests

The LORD examines the righteous…

Psalm 11:5

I spent the year 1983 in Thailand. Although I was on a missionary assignment, I soon discovered I was not as spiritual as I thought I was!

First of all, adjusting to Thailand's three seasons—wet, hot, and hotter—was a challenge. Changing clothes and taking showers three times a day was time consuming. I was grateful our mission insisted we get household help, but the maid and I had communication problems. I really had to hold my tongue when she put bleach in a spray bottle and used it as a stain remover!

I was not accustomed to lizards and cockroaches scurrying across my kitchen counters. Nor did I like the idea of poisonous snakes and scorpions taking up residence in our yard. And when ants invaded during the rainy season, I wanted to scream.

Driving in Bangkok brought out the worst in me. I quickly learned to keep one hand on the horn at all times. I also learned I could give the people I was supposed to be converting dirty looks!

Since I grew up in a home where ministers and missionaries were highly respected, I was appalled by my own behavior. I had no idea I could think such ugly thoughts and that my temper could flare over small things—like the neighborhood guard clanging a bell outside our gate nightly every hour on the hour.

I discussed my frustrations with a seasoned missionary. I was surprised he knew exactly what I was talking about. "I find that my faults have been magnified since I've been here," he told me. "I have to ask God for help more than ever."

Magnified faults. I obviously had more than I realized! In time I came to the conclusion that Thailand was God's exam room for me. He knew I needed to know how I was doing spiritually—and how much I must depend on Him every day.

I found Mrs. Charles E. Cowman's quotation from *Tried by Fire* very encouraging: *"The very fact of trial proves there is something in us very precious to our Lord; else He would not spend so much pain and time on us. Christ would not test us if He did not see the precious ore of faith mingled in the rocky matrix of our nature; and it is to bring this out into purity and beauty that He forces us through the fiery ordeal."*[6]

Perhaps you are suffering today for no other reason than you are being tested. God knows, of course, exactly the what and why of your circumstances, but He may have allowed your trial so that *you* will know how you are doing spiritually.

Two Steps Back

- Have you considered that your trial is perhaps a test?
- How do you feel about being tested so that you can see your spiritual growth—or lack of growth?

Two Steps Forward

- Read James 1:2–17.
- Write down what you consider to be your spiritual weak spots. Make a point to pray about these items.

One Step More

Dear Lord, thank You for trusting me with this trial. If this is a test, help me to pass it! At least, help me to learn what You are trying to teach me. Amen.

Floods

The LORD sits enthroned over the flood;
the LORD is enthroned as King forever.

Psalm 29:10

I prayed a lot for our family's safety during our one year in Thailand. A walled neighborhood and yard, barred windows on our two-level house, and two dogs made us feel somewhat safe. What we weren't prepared for was monsoon season!

The 1983 torrential rains in Bangkok were devastating. Flooded canals spilled murky water into the city's streets, shops, and markets. As we watched the water level rise around our home, we lugged in sandbag after sandbag. The unused entrances (five of them!) were sealed with mud.

We weren't prepared enough. One morning we woke up to knee-deep water in our living room, dining room, and kitchen. We hauled furniture upstairs and moved in with friends who lived in a higher area of the city.

In the seasons of our lives, there are many things for which we are never quite ready: Sickness. Job loss. Financial ruin. Divorce. Death. And even when we prepare for the worst scenario, troubles seem to seep through the cracks.

The prophet Isaiah wrote, "When the enemy comes in like a flood, the Spirit of the Lord will lift up a standard against him" (Isaiah 59:19, NKJ). Satan would love to see you drown in your problems. He wants to block God's purpose for allowing you to wade through a hard time. Don't let him. Remind him that God still "sits enthroned over the flood." He is in control—and He has a plan for you. You *will* reach higher ground with His encouragement and help.

Two Steps Back

- Do you feel you have done your best to "seal the cracks" of your biggest problem?
- Are you finding comfort and help when you read the Bible?

Two Steps Forward

- Read Psalm 29.
- Write in your journal what "the voice of the Lord" means to you.

One Step More

Lord, thank You for watching over me when I feel like I'm drowning. Keep me treading and trusting until I reach the solid ground You are preparing for me. Amen.

Relief

*Answer me when I call to you,
my righteous God.
Give me relief from my distress;
have mercy on me and hear my prayer.*

Psalm 4:1

While living in Thailand, I was surprised when two of my children returned home from bike riding soaking wet. I was shocked when they told me Thais were throwing water balloons at them! But our maid laughed and informed me that the hottest day of the year is considered a holiday. To celebrate, they splash each other (and strangers) with water. They call it *sanuk mak*—"really fun."

It had been a huge adjustment for us to endure March, April, and May, Thailand's hot season. It was common for us to shower three times a day. Air conditioners and fans brought much relief.

So I found it fascinating that the Thai people had the ingenuity to turn one of the most distressful days of the year into a day of celebration (I gave the maid half a day off so she could get wet!).

The Bible says God gives us relief during our times of distress. He knows that we can endure only so much, so He provides special moments when we can forget our pain and fears for a span.

When my father was undergoing a four-bypass open-heart surgery, the family gathered to give him support. His cardiologist had informed us the procedure would be tricky as dad's heart valves had more blockages than he had previously witnessed in his practice. The operation was delayed twice, so we had extra time to worry!

As the hours passed we discovered God was providing relief from the distress we were each experiencing. Mom's brothers and sister paid a visit, and their Irish sense of humor kept us laughing. We prayed, sang, joked with the nurses, and especially enjoyed the family time in the hospital's cafeteria.

Ask God to give you relief from the tension, and then watch for it. Quite often He will give you something to laugh about. You may have to go somewhere to get "splashed on," but it is well worth the effort. Forgetting your problems for even a short while will help you persevere. And remember, the "hot season" will not last forever!

Two Steps Back

- Think about those times when you forgot about your problems momentarily.
- Is there something you can do today to distract you enough to bring some relief?

Two Steps Forward

- Read John 14:27.
- Do something today that will get your mind off of your problems.

One Step More

Dear Lord, thank You for providing breaks in my down times. Please change my attitude toward the pressures in my life. Give me something to celebrate today. Amen.

Perfect Peace

The LORD watches over the foreigner
and sustains the fatherless and the widow…

Psalm 146:9

Living overseas taught me what it feels like to be a foreigner. For starters, I had a great deal to learn about the culture and customs. The language itself was a huge challenge—especially when I tried it out on market vendors! I never did become accustomed to the stares and smirks. In short, it felt strange to be a stranger!

This Psalm says God watches over the strangers. He knows how difficult it is for us to walk into unknown territory, to leave our comfort zones. He's aware that most of us don't function at our max when we're on unfamiliar ground.

Coping with a heartache or tragedy is often like entering a foreign country. You need guidance and assurance as you pass through the unfamiliar life experience. Fortunately, God has promised to be your Protector and Tour Guide—if you will allow Him to be.

As your Protector He will keep evil forces at bay as you try to make sense out of what has happened to you. He will keep you in "perfect peace" (Isaiah 26:3) as you make complicated decisions and face difficult people.

God has far more knowledge about your situation than you do. He is fully aware of every how, when, and why. As your Tour Guide for this journey you never asked to be taken on, He will take you to places you never dreamed possible. He will steer you to answers you cannot imagine. And He will turn this strange experience into a high adventure.

The time I spent in Thailand could have been quite a negative experience if it were not for my language instructors, missionary friends, and helpful neighbors. As you pass through the unfamiliar and tough spots in life, you will find it much easier when you learn to trust God as your Protector and Guide. Only then will you know true peace.

Two Steps Back

- Do you feel out of your comfort zone today?
- What brings you the most peace and assurance right now?

Two Steps Forward

- Read Psalm 55:16–23.
- Make a list of all the ways God is helping you in this "foreign land."

One Step More

Dear God, protect and guide me as I travel through this unfamiliar territory. Even though the journey itself is difficult, help me exchange my fears for Your peace—and explore new possibilities for Your glory. Amen.

A Reason to Sleep

I lie awake, lonely as a solitary sparrow on the roof.

Psalm 102:7 (TLB)

The psalmist who wrote these words must have known something about sparrows.

I often watch these small plain birds from my kitchen window, and I have yet to see one alone. They usually swoop in and out of the yard in large flocks.

Sparrows usually nest and feed off the ground, so a lone one perched on a rooftop at night is not sleeping, eating, or singing. What an accurate picture of loneliness!

The hard times in our lives can breed both loneliness and low self-esteem. Like the author of this verse, we lay awake at night feeling sorry for ourselves. We feel small and unwanted and isolated.

Jesus knows this. "Are not five sparrows sold for two pennies?" He asked His disciples. "Yet not one of them is forgotten by God. Indeed, the very hairs of your head are all numbered. Don't be afraid; you are worth more than many sparrows."

In other words, you don't have to be full of fear and anxiety. You are worth more to God than you can ever imagine. Do you think He is going to forget and forsake someone He values? You may feel like a bird all alone on a deserted rooftop, but He has better plans for you. He wants to help you sleep—and to fly (and dance!) again.

Two Steps Back

- Do you feel loved by God?
- If not, what makes you feel unworthy of His love?

Two Steps Forward

- 1 John 4:7–11.
- Write down what you think it would feel like for someone to love you unconditionally. Now, picture God loving you in the same way.

One Step More

Dear God, just as You keep Your eyes on the sparrows, please watch over me as I sleep. Help me to rest in the warmth of Your love and care. Give me dreams that will inspire me to fly above my problems. Amen.

Knowing God

Great is our Lord and mighty in power;
his understanding has no limit.

Psalm 147:5

When blind Bartimaeus heard Jesus was passing close by him, he cried, "Jesus, Son of David, have mercy on me!" He did not yell, "Jesus, Son of David, I have conjured up enough faith for you to heal me!"

Faith in God is simply having confidence that "great is our Lord and mighty in power." Such a conviction is developed through *knowledge* of Him. And the ways to get to know Him are:

By what others say about Him. Before I first met my husband, Allen, his sister Peggy told me all about him. What she said made me want to meet the man! In the same way, hunger to know God starts by listening to how He has made a difference in others' lives. Classics such as C.S. Lewis' *Mere Christianity* and Lee Strobel's *A Case for Christ* can wet your spiritual appetite.

By what He says about Himself. One weekend Peggy and I stayed at Allen's home while attending a conference in his city. That's when I learned he had once flown airplanes, owned a boat, loved to fish—and traveled. This was some man! Jesus Christ, too, will impress you if you read what He has to say about Himself in the Bible.

By spending time with Him. Allen and I began dating. The more we communicated with each other, the more my confidence in him, and love, grew. It works the same way if you want to know God. Constant communication through prayer is a must.

By committing yourself to Him. On February 26, 1994, Allen and I were married. Our knowledge and confidence in each other took a much deeper dimension. Likewise, faith deepens as you commit yourself to a trustworthy Lord. As you daily ask Him how He wants to live through you, you learn who He really is—and you won't have to conjure up faith.

Two Steps Back

- Where have you received most of your knowledge about God?
- Is the Bible a major source of that knowledge?

Two Steps Forward

- If you don't have a regular plan for reading the Bible, start one today. Begin small. You may want to use a devotional book as a guide or slowly work your way through a book in the New Testament.

- Start a journal entitled, "This is what I know about God." Record those experiences that acquaint you with Him in a fresh way.

One Step More

Lord, please forgive me if I have doubted You in any way. Show me ways to increase my knowledge of You and my faith in You. Amen.

Family Support

*It is God who arms me with strength
and keeps my way secure.*

Psalm 18:32

More than forty years ago I lay in a bed at what was then Metairie, Louisiana's Hospital for Women. I had given birth to a Mardi Gras baby, but my heart was heavy. It had been a difficult birth. Hours of labor. Drugs for pain. I had vague memories of pushing Andrew David into the world. But a nurse immediately wrapped him up and rushed away.

I felt cheated as I watched the other young mothers in my ward cuddling or nursing their newborns. I was told something was wrong with little Andy. He was somewhere in an isolated room, in a big glass box, with tubes all over him. I wasn't allowed to touch him.

"He has the same problem President Kennedy's baby had," the doctor informed me. "At this point, he has a fifty-fifty chance. We're thinking of putting him in an iron lung to transfer him to another hospital."

The President's baby had died.

At that point, I had a choice. I could dwell on the odds—or on God. I kept telling myself that many people were praying. Family, friends, our church. How stunned I was when I walked into the waiting room and found several people from our church—people I didn't know. They were there to just sit and wait for the results with us—and to pray.

Then there was the phone call I made to my parents. It was Wednesday, and I knew that was the night of their church prayer meeting. In my mind, I visualized a bunch of old people praying for our son (when you're twenty-three, anyone over thirty is old!).

Thursday morning we got the good news that in the middle of the night there was an abrupt change in Andy's condition. He went from being on the brink of death to recovery. I clearly believed it had something to do with the old people praying—people who had a lot more faith than I did!

No one is exempt from heartache. We are imperfect beings living in an imperfect world. That's why God had given us a variety of ways to get the support we need when the time comes.

The family of God can be one of the best means of support you will ever receive. Your brothers and sisters in Christ are God's gift to you. Have you accepted this awesome present?

Two Steps Back

- Are you part of a Christian church that makes you feel like family?
- Have you asked those in your community of faith to pray for you?

Two Steps Forward

- Read Romans 15:1–7.
- Make contact with someone in your church. Ask them to pray for you or to place your concerns on a prayer chain or list.

One Step More

Lord, thank you for all my brothers and sisters in Christ. Help me allow them to support me whenever I need an extra boost. And give me Your love for them. Amen.

Go, Pilgrim, Go!

Blessed are those who...have set their hearts on pilgrimage.

Psalm 84:5

A pilgrimage is described in the dictionary as "a journey to a sacred place or shrine" or "any long journey or search, especially one of exalted purpose or moral significance."

There are many places in the world that are connected with some important religious figure or event. It is the custom for many to visit these places for various reasons. Some go to have their sins forgiven. Others hope for a cure of an illness or to gain a special favor. All hope their difficult trip will pay spiritual dividends. People who make these journeys are called pilgrims.

Psalm 84 is a song about taking a spiritual journey. It says that when you yearn to find and know God, you *will* travel through the Valley of Weeping. The good part is that refreshing springs await you on the other side! As you learn and grow from one experience, it will help you to face your next obstacle. You will go from "strength to strength" until your journey is completed.

When you turn your valleys into springs, you create spiritual oases for others. Your faith will inspire them to keep going when it gets tough.

The psalmist reminds us that God gives us all the help we need to make our journey through life—light, protection, grace, and glory! "No good thing will He withhold from those who walk along his paths" (Psa. 84:11, TLB).

Are you in the Valley of Weeping today? Don't quit now. This dark and dangerous place can be the very spot where God wants to create a refreshing spring for His purposes. If you will allow Him to work through these circumstances, someday you will be stronger than you ever believed possible. Keep trekking, Pilgrim!

Two Steps Back

- Have you been in the "Valley of Weeping" before?
- Did you learn and grow from that experience? Did it grow or diminish your faith in God?

Two Steps Forward

- Read Psalm 84.
- Write a letter to God about your present pilgrimage. Bear your soul. Be honest. State your concerns and questions.

One Step More

Dear God, I don't always understand Your ways, but I accept Your wisdom. Thank You for mapping my earthly pilgrimage so that I will grow closer to You. Remind me to help those whose valleys are deeper than mine. Amen.

You Are Unique

A thousand may fall at your side,
ten thousand at your right hand,
but it will not come near you.

Psalm 91:7

Whenever I read this verse, I think of my grandpa Nicholl, or Popsicola, as his grandchildren fondly called him. Since he died when I was quite young, I never really knew this clever, artistic, and sometimes eccentric man.

My mother told me her father did strange things because he was shell-shocked in World War I. She said Popsicola was a good example, however, of Psalm 91:7. Men were killed all around him on the battlefields, but God spared him.

In my child's mind I pictured a young soldier, gun in hand, running alone while thousands died on every side. It made me feel my grandpa was special to God.

Recently I read this verse in a different light. What would have happened if my grandfather had given up when he saw his buddies dying? He could have thought, "What's the use in fighting? I'll just die anyway."

How easy it is to get discouraged when we read the statistics on cancer victims, divorces, drug and alcohol abuse, and on and on. If we are facing something similar, our dreams and hopes can be dashed.

You will do yourself a big favor by not comparing yourself or your situation to what others have experienced. No matter how similar your circumstances are to someone else's—or to the statistics—don't panic. You are unique, and God has His own special plan for you.

My grandfather kept fighting in spite of the odds, and he was protected. God knew he would one day marry and have six children and fourteen grandchildren. And although Popsicola was too poor to patent his many inventions, he passed on his creativity to generations to come.

God has a plan and purpose for your life. Do not be discouraged because thousands have "fallen" by a similar battle. This is God's fight, not yours. He will protect you for His purposes.

Two Steps Back

- Do you believe God has a purpose for your life?
- If so, when and why did you come to this conclusion?

Two Steps Forward

- Read 1 Corinthians 12:12–31.
- Write in your journal what part you play in the Body of Christ.

One Step More

Dear Father, help me focus on Your faithfulness, not my frailty. On Your power, not my pain. On Your strength, not on statistics. Amen.

Dealing with Pain

The LORD has heard my weeping...
the LORD will answer my prayer.

Psalm 6:8, 9 (NLT)

You will recover faster from your heartbreak if you allow yourself to feel the pain associated with it. King David was a man's man, and yet he cried into his pillow every night during a particularly difficult time. It seems even his mattress was soaked!

It's natural to avoid pain. We do this by pushing grief to the back of our minds, keeping busy, turning on music, the television, Facebook, anything to keep the hurt at bay.

Earl Grollman, who wrote twenty-nine books dealing with death, divorce, and suicide, provided grief counseling to family members of Oklahoma City's 168 bomb victims. "Grief can't be rushed," he said in an interview. "You walk through grief, you don't run... Don't mask your despair. Cry when you have to, laugh when you can."[7]

David, who experienced many tragedies throughout his lifetime, didn't hide his hurts. He wrote out his frustrations, composed songs, talked with friends, consulted spiritual leaders, prayed, and even cried a lot.

God has given you vents for the pressures of life. If you refuse to use them, you can slow the healing process and suffer physically and mentally. You may need to set aside time to grieve. Go for a walk. Shut yourself in a room where you won't be disturbed. Think about your loss. Let it sink in—and cry your heart out. Pray.

Ask God to heal your broken heart and help you deal with whatever lies ahead. Then don't be afraid to repeat this exercise. The open wound *will* heal. "The Lord hears my weeping," David concluded after one of his all-night crying sessions. "He listens to my cry for help and will answer my prayer" (Psalm 6:9, Good News).

Two Steps Back

- Have you given yourself permission to experience your pain in its entirety?
- If your answer is no, why not? If your answer is yes, how has it helped you?

Two Steps Forward

- Read Psalm 6.
- Write in your journal the ways that you have dealt with your pain. Be honest.

One Step More

Lord, I want to be healed of this heartache. Thank You for providing ways to release my grief. Give me courage to feel the pain so I can heal faster. Amen.

Symbols of Hope

But now, Lord, what do I look for?
My hope is in you.

Psalm 39:7

Shortly after my first husband and I separated, a friend gave me a stuffed toy rabbit to give me a bit of comfort. I talked and cuddled and cried with that bunny. I kept it on my bed—and named it "Hope." If I could cling to hope, I reasoned, I would survive.

In his book, *A Gift of Hope: How We Survive Our Tragedies,* Dr. Robert Veninga talks about how symbolic gifts can "engender a sense of confidence in the future." He points out, for instance, that a bicycle may be given to a crippled child who is in therapy to walk again. As the youngster visualizes himself pedaling to a friend's house, hope—and determination—set in.[8]

Tangible symbols of hope can be found in dingy prison cells or elaborate cathedrals. Former prisoners of war often tell how a picture, real or imagined, of a spouse or child kindled their will to live. A mosaic of the Good Shepherd can inspire the wounded to trust a loving God. The cross has been a symbol of hope for Christians for centuries.

Why not give yourself a "symbolic gift" to boost your faith? Purchase luggage for when you are well enough to travel. Buy a photo album to keep alive the memory of a departed loved one. Go shopping for a picture of spring flowers or a rising sun to remind yourself this too will pass.

During those dark days, the bunny on my bed often made me smile. When my daughter left home, Hope went with her. It now belongs to her daughter Breyann (who added Faith and Love to her collection!). Someday I will tell her the story of how God used that special gift to remind me of His faithfulness.

Two Steps Back

- Have you ever received a gift that still cheers you up on occasion?
- How do you feel about giving a "gift of hope" to yourself?

Two Steps Forward

- Read Psalm 40:1–5.
- Purchase or make a "symbolic gift of hope" for yourself.

One Step More

Dear God, although life sometimes seems so unfair, help me never to give up. Boost my faith in myself and in You. Please give me creative ideas to keep my hope in Your goodness alive. Amen.

One Loaf in the Boat

When I am afraid, I put my trust in you.

Psalm 56:3

I like the one-loaf-in-the-boat story in the Bible. It seems the disciples forgot to stock up on food while traveling with Jesus. With only one loaf of bread between them, the hungry men thought they had a big problem.

Ironically, they had just witnessed Jesus feeding five thousand men with two loaves of bread and two fish—and four thousand men with only seven loaves and a few small fish! In both cases, there was food to spare. So why were they concerned about their supper with Jesus on board their boat?

Jesus wasn't impressed. "Why are you talking about having no bread?" He asked them. "Do you still not see or understand? Are your hearts hardened? Do you have eyes but fail to see, and ears but fail to hear? And don't you remember" (Mark 8:17–18)?

It seems like a no-brainer, but how often do *we* forget Who is beside us day in and day out? How many times have *we* insulted the Lord by our lack of faith? The same One who fed the thousands, calmed the sea, and cast out demons tells *us*, "Never will I leave you; never will I forsake you" (Hebrews 13:5).

Corrie ten Boom, the famous Christian Holocaust survivor and author, wrote: "Some people think that I have great faith, but that is not true. I do not have great faith—I have faith in a great God!"[9]

When you focus on the goodness and greatness of the Lord instead of your fears, wonderful things will happen. The secret is to remember He's in your boat!

Two Steps Back

- Do you believe God is with you at all times—or that He comes and goes?
- When do you sense His presence the most?

Two Steps Forward

- Read Mark 8:13–21.
- Read Psalm 139.

One Step More

Dear Lord, forgive me if I have insulted You by my lack of faith. Thank You for being in my boat today. I know with You beside me, I can weather any storm. Amen.

Decisions

*Teach me knowledge and good judgment,
for I trust your commands.*

Psalm 119:66

Whenever you encounter a crisis, you must make decisions. If you lose a job, a decision about how to generate income arises. If a marriage fails, you choose a new way of life. When a loved one dies, a funeral must be arranged and an estate be settled. If health fails, there are the ins and outs of medical care. The decisions you are called to make during these times can be monumental and life changing. They also can keep you awake at night!

Sometimes a crisis is the jolt we need to wake up and smell the coffee—or the roses. Often God positions us where we are forced to make changes. If life carried on pretty much the same day after day, year after year, most of us would just keep trucking and stagnate.

Joshua was a man who knew a great deal about tragedies and triumphs and the choices they require. As Moses's assistant, he witnessed the many decisions that were required to lead the Israelites out of Egypt and through a wilderness in obedience to God. When he became the man in charge following Moses's death, he had the responsibility of leading thousands across the Jordan River and conquering the Promised Land by military force. Facing death as an old man, he told the Israelites to make the greatest choice of all: to serve God or to serve the false gods that surrounded them in their new land.

If you want to sleep at night, ask God for "knowledge and good judgment" in making the decisions ahead of you. Your best ideas will probably come when you are rested and renewed by a good night's sleep. Make it a habit not to allow yourself to think about your problems once your head is on your pillow. Sleep is your time-out—and you deserve it.

Two Steps Back

- Are you in a place right now where important decisions are pending?
- If so, have you prayed about those decisions?

Two Steps Forward

- Read James 3:13–17.
- If you can't sleep because of decisions that must be made, make a list of those concerns and then determine to deal with them in the morning.

One Step More

Dear God, help me to realize that Your peace is the best sleeping pill out there. Right now I ask You to give me direction in all the decisions I must make—tomorrow. Tonight I'm going to sleep. Amen.

Determination

As for me, I trust in You, O Lord.

Psalm 31:14 (NKJ)

As I read through the New King James Version of the Psalms, a phrase caught my attention: "As for me." Here are some other examples aside from our verse today:

As for me, I will see Your face...
As for me, You uphold me...
As for me, I will call upon God...
As for me, my prayer is to You.[10]

To me, those three little words speak volumes. A longer form of them would be: "The rest of you can do what you want to do, but as far as I'm concerned..." I call it making a decision—or *determination.*

The Vancouver Sun once carried a story in its careers section about Toni Beor, a young single mother who made an amazing comeback after ill health forced her off work:

"A decade ago, she was living in a tiny basement apartment in Renfrew, Ont., a single mother with a very young son and no child support. Today, she produces high-end tailoring under her own designer label, holds the contract for designing and manufacturing the uniforms for the staff of the Royal York Hotel in Toronto, and runs her own boutique and factory.... In 1991, she had one sewing machine, an iron, several years of training in tailoring from her native England, and little else except determination."[11]

Abraham Lincoln once said, "Most people are about as happy as they make up their minds to be." Determination is simply making up your mind and setting a course for yourself. Solutions to problems won't materialize by themselves.

The combination of resolution and faith is unbeatable. The Psalmist made firm decisions to get moving—with God's help. Old Testament Joshua had the same resolve: "Choose for yourselves this day whom you will serve... but as for me and my house, we will serve the Lord" (Joshua 24:15, NKJ). Determination plus God is your best mix for success.

Two Steps Back

- Do you think of yourself as a strong, determined person—or wishy-washy?
- What do you think would motivate you to become more strong-minded about doing the right thing?

Two Steps Forward

- Read Psalm 71.
- Complete this statement: As for ME, I will

_____

_____

_____

One Step More

Dear God, help me make decisions today that will bring me closer to You and to Your plan for my life. Guide my steps as I choose faith over fear. Amen.

Sword or Savior?

I put no trust in my bow,
my sword does not bring me victory;
but you give us victory over our enemies,
you put our adversaries to shame.

Psalm 44:6–7

Attending Bible college was my childhood dream. Influenced by missionary relatives and books about missionary adventures, I desperately wanted to be one. I was elated—and frightened—when at age eighteen, I was accepted into a small Canadian college.

I had scraped together enough money from a summer job and some parental assistance for the first semester. When I arrived on campus, however, I discovered the tuition and other fees were more than I had anticipated. After giving the registrar the required amount, I had only change left.

Sitting on my bunk, I clung to those few coins. It was a defining moment for me. I could phone home for help, but it seemed like cheating. I was on a spiritual solo flight, and I had to start trusting God—just like the missionaries.

That morning I received a letter from my sister Carolyn. I took it, along with my Bible, to the college chapel to read in private. Beneath her sprawling signature, Carolyn penned, "Read Philippians 4:19." I got goose bumps when I read, "My God shall supply all your need according to his riches in glory by Christ Jesus."[12] I got on my knees and begged God for that to be true!

On the way back to my room, the dorm phone rang as I walked by it. A lady who lived near the college needed a babysitter. Of course, I volunteered! That job eventually led to more in her home—and at her neighbor's. It was exactly what I needed for my first financial crisis!

God answered many of my desperate prayers at that college. Those experiences taught me that He is reliable. Like the Psalmist who trusted God instead of his sword, I learned to depend on God instead of my parents.

It's easy to rely on something or someone other than God. For one thing, we can't see Him. And in our difficulties, He may seem far away or even non-existent. But victory may elude us until we recognize our dependencies as a lack of faith.

Two Steps Back

- Do you have a "sword" you depend on more than you should?
- Do you depend on your spouse, a friend, money, a career, or your own strength more than God?

Two Steps Forward

- Make a list of the possible "swords" you are using to fight your battles.
- Read Psalm 44:1–8.

One Step More

Lord, show me if I am depending on something or someone more than You. Help me to remember that Your way is always best. Amen.

Pity Parties

Why, my soul, are you downcast?
Why so disturbed within me?
Put your hope in God,
for I will yet praise him,
my Savior and my God.

Psalm 42:5

In her book, *To Live Again,* Catherine Marshall tells the story of an unusual visit she received while bedridden with tuberculosis. Anita, a sophisticated and wealthy friend, marched into her bedroom one day.

"Catherine," she declared, "you've been on my mind for days. I've been tempted to feel sorry for you. I'll be damned if I'll feel sorry for you. Forgive the language, but I feel just that vehemently about it. Pity wouldn't help you a bit. Besides, why should I pity you? You have all you need—the strength and guidance of God."

Catherine said her friend's words were like ice water striking her in the face. But instead of resenting them, they made her feel suddenly alive. They gave her the courage to think, "All right, don't pity me... I'm going to get out of here!"[13]

When we first encounter a tragedy, God is gentle with us in the same way a parent consoles a hurting child. There comes a time, however, when He lets us know that it's time to quit feeling sorry for ourselves and get on with the program. His way is not to lessen the problem but to build up our resources.

Someone else said, "Self-pity is a prison without walls—a sign pointing to nowhere." Whenever people refuse to stop feeling sorry for themselves, they are only adding more pain to their suffering. They are also isolating themselves from the help they so desperately need. They become "stuck in bitterness."

If you are a member of the poor-me club, you can turn in your card. It may not be easy, but you won't regret it. Start now by looking for the good in your life. Catherine Marshall concluded: "Gratitude is a sure cure for self-pity—that special illness at the heart of all grief." And remember you, too, have the strength and guidance of God.

Two Steps Back

- When have you been tempted to feel sorry for yourself?
- Are you having a pity party today?

Two Steps Forward

- Read Psalm 103.
- Make a list of all the things for which you can be thankful.

One Step More

Dear Father, forgive me if I have spent too much time and energy feeling sorry for myself. Thank You for all the good things You have brought my way. Please help me to abandon any pity party I'm tempted to attend. Keep me happy in You. Amen.

Shakes and Shocks

Therefore we will not fear, though the earth give way
and the mountains fall into the heart of the sea,
though its waters roar and foam
and the mountains quake with their surging.

Psalm 46:2–3

My friend Bonnie kept a little, flowered suitcase on her bed for years. It contained a flashlight, radio, cell phone, money, and her best jewelry. Every night at bedtime Bonnie dumped the contents of her purse and the jewelry she was wearing into this bag. She also kept a sweatshirt, pair of jeans, runners, and socks near her bed.

Bonnie's strange behavior had merit. On January 17, 1994, at 4:32 a.m., she and her husband became victims of the terrifying Los Angeles earthquake. The memory of waking suddenly to monstrous jolts, thunderous noise, and destruction everywhere was difficult to shake. Recalling how helpless she felt, Bonnie wanted to be better prepared should it happen again.

We live in the Vancouver, British Columbia area—which is on the same Cascadian subduction zone as Los Angeles. Although the media has warned everyone to prepare for a large earthquake, only a small percentage has complied. We are like those James mentioned, who say, "Today or tomorrow we will go to this or that city, spend a year there, carry on business and make money." The apostle warned that nobody knows what will happen tomorrow. He said it is more appropriate to say, "If it is the Lord's will, we will live and do this or that" (James 4:13–15).

You may have just experienced the worst "quake" in your life or feel you are presently on unsettled ground. The verse preceding our scripture today says, "God is our refuge and strength, an ever-present help in trouble" (Psa. 46:1). There is no reason to live in fear if you really believe this. Keeping focused on God instead of your circumstances will settle you. Try it today.

Two Steps Back

- When was the last time you felt "settled?"
- What do you think made you feel secure at that time?

Two Steps Forward

- Read Psalm 46.
- Write out Psalm 46:1 and display it in a prominent place.

One Step More

Dear Father, I acknowledge that I cannot control many of the circumstances around me. Thank You for Your promise to be my refuge and strength today. Should I feel my world shake, keep me steady. Amen.

Faith for Rice

*The eyes of all look to you,
and you give them their food at the proper time.*

Psalm 145:15

Hudson Taylor was only twenty-one when he sailed from England to China as a missionary doctor. He soon discovered that the support from his mission was unreliable, and trusting God alone for his needs was his best option.

The young man's faith was tested over and over. He traveled by foot, canal, boat, and even wheelbarrow into areas no other missionary had dared venture. He slept in local inns, cheap lodgings, or wherever he could lay his head. He did the unheard of by dressing like the Chinese in order to win their acceptance. He evangelized and tended the sick wherever he went, trusting God to supply the need for every task.

Hudson had been in China about six years when he was asked to take over a new hospital from a doctor who returned to Scotland after his wife's death. The hospital was on shaky financial ground from the very start, and there was no sense of where funding to keep it running would come from. Hudson's response was: "A brand new hospital in running order shouldn't lie empty. If it's God's will to keep it open, He will provide the means."

One day the hospital's cook said to the doctor, "We have opened the last bag of rice"—to which Hudson replied, "Then the Lord's time must surely be near to meet our need."

He was right. A letter soon arrived from a friend in England. "I have inherited a legacy from my father," the author wrote. "I shall not be altering my standard of living. The enclosed fifty pounds is to be used at your discretion. Will you kindly indicate how more can be used?"[14]

Are you on your "last bag of rice?" Have your resources dwindled to the point where you don't know what you are going to do next? Have you run out of options? Well, "the Lord's time must surely be near" to meet your need! His timing is always perfect—and He knows the price of your "rice."

Two Steps Back

- Think back to an answered prayer.
- Have you ever had a prayer answered just in the nick of time?

Two Steps Forward

- Write out the details of a concern today.
- Read Matthew 6:25–34.

One Step More

Lord, You know all about my circumstances today. Your solution and timing will be perfect, so please help me not to give up. Amen.

Easy Street

Happy is he who has the God of Jacob for his help.

Psalm 146:5 (NKJ)

I was enjoying a morning stroll when I noticed the first house on "Easy Street." The large old home with peeling paint and overgrown grass was leaning to one side. A big sleepy-eyed dog guarded a sagging porch. The other houses didn't look much better.

You would think luxury homes and manicured lawns would line a street with such a name, and yet that scene mirrored reality. The quality of life often deteriorates when things become too soft, too uncomplicated. Unfortunately, it sometimes takes a wake-up call to make us realize our shingles need a paint job!

Jacob lived the prime years of his life on "Easy Street." While his twin brother, Esau, hunted and farmed for a living, Jacob relaxed in his tents. His mother indulged him. He even convinced Esau, who was famished at the time, to trade him his birthright for a pot of stew.

Jacob's pursuit of happiness through deceit was short-lived. When he heard Esau was planning to murder him, he became a fugitive. His wake-up call came one night while using a rock for a pillow.

God told Jacob in a dream that he would become the father of a great nation. "I am with you and will watch over you wherever you go, and I will bring you back to this land. I will not leave you until I have done what I have promised you" (Genesis 28:15).

When Jacob woke up, he made a bargain with God. If He would help him return home in peace by protecting him and providing him with food and clothes, then he would serve Him and give Him ten percent of his income.

Perhaps you can remember a time when life was pleasant and uncomplicated. You may have lived on "Easy Street" and never dreamed your life would be what it is today. Maybe you've been handed problems you never asked for or deserved. In any case, you've been jolted into the realization that you need help.

Remember, "the God of Jacob" is on your side. Not only did God forgive Jacob for his deceitfulness and laziness, but He also promised him a great future. Just think! No matter how messed up you may be, God will be merciful if you place your trust in Him. He doesn't guarantee you'll live on "Easy Street," but He does promise you forgiveness, protection, provision, and guidance. That certainly will make your life less stressful!

Two Steps Back

- Has there been a time in your life when you felt you were living on "Easy Street?"
- How would you describe your life now?

Two Steps Forward

- Read Proverbs 14:10–14.
- Write in your journal the possible reasons why God has allowed you to be where you are today.

One Step More

Lord, forgive me if I have been lazy or complacent. Thank You for second chances. Help me to receive all You have for me in order to bless You and others. Amen.

Miracles

In the day of my trouble I will
call upon You, for You will answer me.

Psalm 86:7 (NKJ)

My three children were preschoolers when I encountered a big "day of trouble." I awoke one morning to the stark realization that, like Mother Hubbard, my cupboards were bare.

I checked—and rechecked—the refrigerator and pantry. There was only enough food in the house for breakfast. Nothing more. Not even flour to make bread.

After feeding the boys, I sent them upstairs to play. As I put the baby down for her morning nap, I prayed. Boy, did I pray!

I had no idea what I'd do if my husband's due-to-arrive salary was not in our mailbox by noon. He was out of town, and there was no way to contact him.

But the mailman came and went, leaving only bills behind. I knew then that my faith was on the line. Did God really "supply all your needs" like the Bible promised, or was I naive to believe it?

Just when I was beginning to think that maybe God was one big hoax, there was a light rap on my front door. It was eleven o'clock.

When I opened it I stared in disbelief. There on the porch, lined in a neat row, were four boxes of groceries!

A young woman explained she'd been asked to drop them off since she was coming into town. As it turned out, the benefactors lived almost a hundred miles from us, and we hardly knew them. When I later examined the boxes' contents, I could have sworn whoever bought the food had a copy of my grocery list!

I will never forget the fear that gripped me that morning over forty years ago now. Nor will I ever forget that awesome moment when I opened my door and came face to face with a miracle.

Maybe you need a miracle today. God has not forgotten you. You can place yourself entirely in His hands, knowing He loves you and wants what is best for you.

His way and timing are perfect. When you need it most, and maybe when you least expect it, you will hear a rap on your door. The answer may be entirely different from what you've imagined, but it will be the right one.

Two Steps Back

- Do you believe miracles can still happen today?
- Have you ever experienced one?

Two Steps Forward

- Ask someone you admire for their spiritual qualities to relate a miracle that has happened to them.
- Read Matthew 9:18–32.

One Step More

Dear Father, thank You for keeping Your promises. Please increase my faith so that I can do Your will. Forgive me for not always believing when I should. Amen.

Your Intercessor

*You have been my defense
and refuge in the day of trouble.*

Psalm 59:16 (NKJ)

I received this e-mail from a friend one morning after writing her concerning my fears for my health: "*Do not give up on God... He did not bring you this far to let you fall. Take heart, Jesus says He is praying for you.*"

What a great thought! Whenever I find myself facing a crisis, I immediately contact people I know who are good at praying. What better person to pray for me than Jesus Himself!

Does Jesus really pray for us? I did some searching in the Bible and discovered He does indeed pray for us, especially for those who belong to Him.

Did you know Jesus prayed for you long before you were born? Shortly before He was crucified, He spent a great deal of time interceding for His disciples—and for future believers: "My prayer is not for them (disciples) alone. I pray also for those who will believe in me through their message..." (John 17:20).

And He prays for you now:

"He (Christ) entered heaven itself, now to appear for us in God's presence" (Hebrews 9:24).

"If anybody does sin, we have one who speaks to the Father in our defense—Jesus Christ, the Righteous One" (1 John 2:1).

"Therefore he is able to save completely those who come to God through him, because he always lives to intercede for them" (Hebrews 7:25).

The thought of Jesus praying for *you* should make you feel loved and secure. When you can't put into words your fears and frustrations, He knows exactly what to say on your behalf. He will always ask for the Father's best for you.

Two Steps Back

- Have you ever thought about Jesus praying for you?
- How does this truth make you feel?

Two Steps Forward

- Read Hebrews 7:20–28.
- Make a list in your journal entitled "Things I Want Jesus to Pray For."

One Step More

Dear Father, thank You for providing a way for me to have a personal relationship with You through Jesus, Your Son. And thank You for listening to His prayers for me. Right now I need all the help I can get. In Jesus's name, Amen.

Open Wide!

I am the LORD your God...
Open wide your mouth and I will fill it.

Psalm 81:10

Janet, a young friend, was attractive, smart, and ambitious. She was a career woman bent on proving herself in her profession, and outwardly she seemed happy.

One day she expressed to me that something was missing in her life. She said she thought she'd be happy once she got to the top of her career, but she discovered it didn't work that way. She asked if I thought it might have something to do with her spiritual side.

I was happy to point Janet toward a personal relationship with Jesus Christ as the only source of true happiness and fulfillment. I gave her a Bible and some Christian books, hoping she would read her way to Truth—and live happily ever after.

I'm not sure what Janet read, but she later told me she wasn't sure she could hand her life over to Christ. I asked her why she was so afraid.

"What if He tells me I can't get married or have children?" she asked. "And what if He wants me to be a missionary in some foreign country?"

I assured Janet that God loved her, and would never ask her to do anything that He couldn't help her do. I told her that she needed to trust Him first, and only then would she experience His peace and goodness in her life.

Our verse today tells us to open our spiritual mouth WIDE and let God fill it. This takes an act of faith. It's like being blindfolded and told to taste an unknown substance. You have to believe that you won't be fed something awful-tasting, rotten, or poisonous.

Jesus said: "My purpose is to give life in all its fullness. I am the Good Shepherd. The Good Shepherd lays down his life for the sheep" (John 10:10–11, TLB). You certainly can trust someone who is willing to die for you!

Janet did eventually give her life to Jesus Christ. It has brought me tremendous pleasure to witness what He is doing in her and through her. You, too, can experience His fullness if you will be opened—and the wider the better!

Two Steps Back

- Is fear keeping you from experiencing God's best?
- Are you willing to "open your mouth wide" and allow Him to feed you with His goodness?

Two Steps Forward

- Read Matthew 6:25–34. Write down the reasons that may be keeping you from "feeding on God's faithfulness."
- Mention each one of these reasons to God, and ask for His help and guidance.

One Step More

Dear God, help me open my spiritual mouth in faith, knowing You want to feed me with Your goodness. Help me to trust You more. Amen.

Mind Overload

My heart meditated and my spirit asked:
"Will the Lord reject forever?
Will he never show his favor again?"

Psalm 77:6–7

As you struggle with your crisis or heartbreak, you will experience a tremendous need to think through what has happened—or is happening—to you. You may find yourself examining certain details over and over again. You will look at them from various angles. You may try to find answers through reading or searching the Internet.

When Mary discovered her adult son had multiple sclerosis, her mind and emotions worked overtime. Perplexed and deeply concerned, she talked with anyone she knew who had a family member with MS. She searched for information online. And she thought and thought about how this could possibly happen in a family with very few health problems. She began to lose sleep.

"Thinking through" helps us to feel in control. If we could only come up with some answers, we might be able to find a solution or make some sense in our dilemma.

God has given you a mind to use. The thought process can be very helpful in sorting out facts, making decisions, and taking appropriate action. You must be cautious, however, of over-thinking or of allowing negative thoughts to dominate your reasoning process.

Our scripture today talks about meditating, or thinking, but it also says you should allow your *spirit* to help you search for answers. If you are in tune with God's Spirit, your thought patterns are more likely to go in a correct direction.

"For my thoughts are not your thoughts, neither are your ways my ways," declares the LORD. "As the heavens are higher than the earth, so are my ways higher than your ways, and my thoughts than your thoughts" (Isaiah 55:9).

Let God do the bulk of the thinking for you. This doesn't imply you can make mindless decisions, but rather emphasizes the importance of concentrating on God's thoughts instead of your own.

As you allow your spiritual side to do a "diligent search," you will find not just answers, but right answers. You will also be able to sleep better at night knowing that an all-loving and all-knowing God is in control. Think about that!

Two Steps Back

- Are you trying to think things through as a way of controlling your current situation?
- Have you asked God what He thinks about it?

Two Steps Forward

- Read Isaiah 55.
- Make a conscious effort to think in a more positive and faith-filled way.

One Step More

Dear God, thank You for my mind and for my ability to think. Help me to use this tool properly. Forgive me if I have tried to figure everything out on my own. Please give me Your thoughts on this matter—and help me to accept what You will tell me. Amen.

Fighting Fear

*I sought the LORD, and he answered me;
he delivered me from all my fears.*

Psalm 34:4

In his book, *The Gift of Fear: Survival Signals That Protect Us from Violence,* Gavin de Becker says, *"True fear is a signal in the presence of danger, whereas unwarranted fear is a waste of time. True fear is based on perceptions from your environment. Unwarranted fear is based on your imagination or memory."*[15]

Unfounded fears distort reality and make a situation worse than what it is. My friend Jean, for instance, was a basket case for three days after learning something was amiss on her mammogram. "I went through hell," she told me. "I have an active imagination and had my grave dug." Her x-ray had been misread!

Someone said fear is **F**alse **E**vidence **A**ppearing **R**eal. A good one to remember!

Keep in mind that fear is an emotion and not necessarily a reality. Thought patterns can be changed. "For God has not given us a spirit of fear, but of power and of love and of a sound mind" (2 Tim. 1:7, NKJ). With God's help, you can discipline your mind to think truthful and powerful thoughts rather than negative and fearful ones.

Someone said, "Courage is being bold in spite of your fears." When my mother told me how frightened she was to give a workshop at a women's retreat, I told her to stand tall, hold her head high, and talk with confidence. In other words, act as if she wasn't afraid. She took my advice and gave a successful speech.

So work on your faith. There is no verse in the Bible that calms my fears more than, "You will keep him in perfect peace, whose mind is stayed on You, because he trusts in You" (Isaiah 26:3, NKJ). Instead of dwelling on your fears, think about what a loving and mighty God you have. Read your Bible. Pray. Talk over your apprehensions with a Christian whose faith you admire. The more room you give God in your life, the less space there will be for fear. And you should sleep better.

Two Steps Back

- Think about specific fears that may be keeping you awake at night.
- How likely are these fears to come true?

Two Steps Forward

- Read 2 Timothy 1:7–12.
- Contact a Christian mentor to discuss your biggest fear.

One Step More

Dear God, forgive me if I have allowed fear to control me. Thank You for Your love and faithfulness. Keep my mind on You instead of my apprehensions. Amen.

A Thanksgiving Offering

*I will sacrifice a thank offering to you
and call on the name of the LORD.*

Psalm 116:17

For weeks I knew something was wrong with me. My stomach had bloated to the point that I appeared to be pregnant. Nothing significant was showing up from the tests my doctor ordered.

One day, out of frustration, I broke down and sobbed, "God, I don't know what is wrong with me, but please help me!"

That day I read from the Bible, "In everything give thanks; for this is the will of God in Christ Jesus for you" (1 Thess. 5:18, NKJ). And the verse for my daily devotional was, "And whatever you do, whether in word or deed, do it all in the name of the Lord Jesus, giving thanks to God the Father through Him" (Col. 3:17).

Hearing about thankfulness twice in one day made me think! However, it seemed rather silly. Wouldn't I be displaying a lack of faith by thanking God for my bloated abdomen? And yet I couldn't deny what I had read.

So I placed my right hand on my protruding belly and prayed: "Lord, I don't know why this has happened to me, but I thank You for it." Peace followed. It didn't make sense, but I felt I had done the right thing.

A couple weeks later I learned I had ovarian cancer. My gynecologist told me that if my stomach had not been bloated, the tumor would have continued to grow unchecked. My "condition" had made it possible for the cancer to be detected at an early stage!

Praising God while in pain can be difficult. It's called "sacrificing a thank offering." It's an act of faith. Even if you can't say the words with confidence, it will be a step in the right direction: God's will for you.

Two Steps Back

- What can you be thankful for today?
- Are you willing to thank God for something that doesn't make sense?

Two Steps Forward

- Read Psalm 100.
- Write out a list of things you are truly thankful for.

One Step More

Dear Lord, I thank You for _____, although I don't understand why this is happening. Please give me the help I need to accept Your perfect will. Amen.

I AM

Be still, and know that I am God.

Psalm 46:10

I was sitting in my doctor's examining room, waiting for him to tell me the results of an ultrasound. It was five days before Christmas 1999, and I looked like I was five months pregnant.

Dr. Wright wasn't his cheery self when he entered the room. "It doesn't look good," he almost whispered as he thumbed through my file. "We've found a fairly large tumor growing on your left ovary."

The pinched look on his face frightened me.

"Ovarian cancer?" I almost choked on the words.

"It's a possibility," he answered. "I've booked you to see a gynecologist first thing tomorrow morning."

Tomorrow seemed an eternity away as I drove home from his office that afternoon. To say I was frightened would be an understatement. I was terrified.

That evening Allen tried to console me. He prayed for me, but I felt like he was talking to the walls. I did try to locate an inspirational poem given me a year before by a breast cancer survivor. I thought it might help, but I couldn't find it.

Ten days later I was in the hospital. The night before my surgery, Allen handed me a get-well card from missionary friends in Sri Lanka. When I opened it, a smaller card fell out. I began to cry. It was the poem I had been searching for! I read:

I was regretting the past
and fearing the future.
Suddenly my Lord was speaking:
"My name is I AM."
He paused.
I waited. He continued,
"When you live in the past
with its mistakes and regrets,
it is hard. I am not there.
My name is not I WAS.

When you live in the future,
with its problems and fears,
it is hard. I am not there.
My name is not I WILL BE.

When you live in this moment,
it is not hard. I am here.
My name is I AM."

Helen Mallicoat[16]

I faced my surgery with peace and confidence. And it didn't surprise me when Dr. Robson later gave me the good news that the cancer had not spread beyond the tumor.

I have no idea what you are facing today, but God is trustworthy. The Great I AM is with you this very moment—and He won't forsake you tomorrow.

Two Steps Back

- What worries you the most today?
- What is the worst possible scenario that could happen in this situation?

Two Steps Forward

- Read John 14:25–31.
- Write down your main concerns, mention each one to God—and then throw the list in the garbage.

One Step More

Father, right now I quiet myself in Your presence. Forgive me for hanging onto the failures and hurts of my past. Give me courage to face the future. And help me to live only in the present moment—one day at a time. Amen.

Sleeping Pill

With long life I will satisfy him,
and show him my salvation.

Psalm 91:16

As I drove home from the doctor's office after just hearing, "If you lived in the States, you'd be operated on tomorrow," I could only think of two people I wanted to call with the news that I probably had ovarian cancer—my sister Carolyn, and Edna, an older friend and spiritual mentor. Both women were out that evening, but I connected with them the next day.

I later phoned my parents, my sister Gloria, and my closest friends, but I know now that God directed me to Carolyn for special emotional and prayer support—and to Edna to help me sleep at night!

Edna and I had once attended the same church, but now we connected mainly through Christmas cards. I didn't know that Edna had herself been diagnosed with ovarian cancer only a few years prior to me. Her seven-year battle with the disease was a private and fierce spiritual journey. After being pronounced cured by her doctor, she encouraged others with her testimony.

Edna prayed with me over the phone, and then gave me some advice that helped put me to sleep—literally! "Read Psalm 91 every night," she told me. At that point I was relying on a sleeping pill to knock me out, and this sounded like a much better prescription.

So every night I read Psalm 91 before I removed my contact lenses. Over and over I read about God as my fortress, my refuge, my dwelling. I devoured the positive promises of God to

81

protect, provide, and bring peace. I especially liked the last verse that promised a long life! The faith-building verses definitely gave me the peace I needed to doze off.

Why don't *you* try Psalm 91 as *your* sleeping pill?

Two Steps Back

- Are your thoughts keeping you awake at night?
- If so, how many of these thoughts are connected to fear?

Two Steps Forward

- Read Psalm 91 before bedtime every night for a week— or for as long as you need to.
- Write in your journal the promises of God in Psalm 91 that apply to you.

One Step More

Dear God, thank You for Your promise to be always with me no matter what. Help me to sleep tonight, confident that You are watching over me and all that concerns me. Amen.

Family

*How good and pleasant it is
when God's people live together in unity!*

Psalm 133:1

A crisis changes families. Sometimes families become more loving, more caring. When I was diagnosed with cancer, my adult children were wonderful. They became more verbal about their love for me. They put aside their own plans to accommodate my doctor and hospital appointments. They became experts on ovarian cancer.

But some families do not function well under pressure. They become uptight. Frustrations build. Tempers flare. Accusations fly. When communication remains blocked, relationships begin to break.

A crisis may fracture a family for various reasons. Most of us are unskilled in dealing with the unexpected. We do not plan on heartbreaks, and interaction with one another can be one of the most difficult aspects of the whole situation.

The need to find out who is responsible for a tragedy also can sever a family. Someone is blamed. Anger builds. Retaliation escalates. Past hurts surface. Family members know each other's weaknesses—and which buttons to push to manipulate or aggravate one another.

What can you do to help your family stay intact during this difficult time? Remember it is God's will for you to "live together in unity." Ask for His help in dealing with each family member. Accept what has happened, and go on from there.

In his book, *A Gift of Hope: How We Survive Our Tragedies,* Dr. Robert Veninga says, "Those who accept conflict and address their problems in a rational manner are able to find solutions enabling them to move into a new era; those who can't, find that their families splinter apart."[17]

He suggests family conferences, giving each other space and unconditional love, and becoming a model yourself of "competence, rationality, and hope." Even if you are at the center of the tragedy, you can, with God's help, create unity among those you love.

Two Steps Back

- How is your crisis affecting individual family members?
- Are you able to communicate to them your opinions and frustrations?

Two Steps Forward

- Read Jeremiah 31:16–17.
- Pray for each family member who may be affected by your circumstances.

One Step More

Dear God, please help those I love understand that this crisis is temporary. Help all of us use it to build our love for You and for each other. May good win over evil, and keep us together as a family. Amen.

Night Watches

On my bed I remember you;
I think of you through the watches of the night.

Psalm 63:6

This morning I was reading near a window when I noticed a chickadee having a shower in our apple tree. Instead of seeking shelter from the rain, the little bird was busy cleaning himself directly under the drizzle. While I was glad to be dry, he was taking advantage of our downpour!

When David wrote the sixty-third Psalm, he was hiding from his enemies in the wilderness of Judea. He no doubt had many sleepless nights. Using the long nights to think and pray was his "shower in the rain."

I learned the secret of taking advantage of a bad situation while undergoing treatment for cancer. Confined to a recliner shortly after surgery, I used the time to read, write, and pray. "I can't help envying you," a friend told me—while she dusted my furniture!

When I learned my particular chemotherapy would cause hair loss, I went wig shopping with a friend. Trying on new hairstyles was great fun, and my husband loved his "new woman."

My health loss opened the door for me to learn about cancer first-hand. Weight loss gave me the opportunity to fit into some favorite old clothes. Sleep loss made it possible for me to pray more. In short, taking advantage of the disadvantages provided me with one of the greatest weapons to fight the disease—positive thinking.

Our verse today as presented in *The Message* reads*: "If I'm sleepless at midnight, I spend the hours in grateful reflection."*[18] The next time you find it difficult to sleep, try thanking God for what blessings remain in your life. It may not make you doze, but it will give you a measure of peace.

Two Steps Back

- Have you tried to use your times of sleeplessness for prayer?
- Have you been able to steer your mind to positive ideas and prayers of gratitude?

Two Steps Forward

- Read Psalm 3:4–8.
- Make a list of things for which you are thankful. Put this list beside your bed for those times when you can't sleep.

One Step More

Dear God, You know how I long for sleep, and for strength to carry on. And You know the cause of my insomnia. Help me, like the psalmist, to use this time for prayer and grateful reflection. Amen.

Support

*Then the righteous will gather about me
because of your goodness to me.*

Psalm 142:7

After my last chemotherapy treatment, I felt like a child released to the playground for recess. Three days later, however, I was fatigued and depressed. Negative thoughts plagued me. What if the chemo and radiation weren't enough? What would I do if the cancer returned? Why didn't so-and-so phone me? Maybe everyone had stopped praying...

For several days I indulged in self-pity, something I had promised myself I wouldn't do. I felt abandoned by God. Where was all the faith and fortitude I had during my surgery and first chemo treatments? Why did my prayers seem flat, His presence far away?

Then one afternoon I received a letter, written on pink stationery, from a friend. Halfway down the first page she wrote: "I want to leave this verse with you: 'My Presence will go with you, and I will give you rest'" (Exodus 33:14).

I then opened a card from another friend. She wrote: "Cathy, my heart is touched by your illness and how very brave you are. You do have a world of people who love you and really care."

I stared at the words on the letter and card. Had Jesus just walked into the room and handed me the answer to my questions?

Later in the day I received a call from my friends Glen and Kay, a retired gynecologist and his wife. I appreciated their knowledge of my "case" and their prayers. Talking with them brought more comfort.

By the end of the day my tiredness and sadness had lifted. I knew the Lord had communicated His love and care for me through concerned Christians.

When you can't see tangible evidence of God working, don't forget He uses others to help you. If you watch and listen closely enough, you will see Him and hear Him through a Christian friend, pastor, or counselor. Jesus said: "Ask and it will be given unto you; seek and you will find; knock and the door will be opened to you" (Matthew 7:7).

If your mailbox is empty, try knocking on someone's door.

Two Steps Back

- Who has given you the most support through all of this?
- Are you angry with someone for not being more supportive?

Two Steps Forward

- Read Psalm 145:14–21.
- Make a list of those who have supported you through this ordeal. Thank God for each of them by name.

One Step More

Dear Lord, forgive me if I have indulged in self-pity today. Thank You for reminding me that You use others to pray for me and help me when I need it the most. Amen.

Mighty Medicine

*Our mouths were filled with laughter,
our tongues with songs of joy.*

Psalm 126:2

Someone said, "A sense of humor helps us overlook the unbecoming, understand the unconventional, tolerate the unpleasant, overcome the unexpected, and outlast the unbearable."

When I was undergoing treatments for cancer, one friend sent me stacks of jokes and humorous stories with her get-well cards. She knew laughter is a gift from God that helps us through the not-so-funny times. It is "the shock absorber that eases the blows of life."

When my hair fell out due to chemotherapy, I knew I had a choice. I could either become frustrated or depressed, or I could make the best of it. I believe my decision to laugh as much as possible through the ordeal paid off.

"I'm looking like my dad more and more," I'd say to friends—or—"I'm going to soar through this like an eagle—a bald eagle!"

My friend Karen brought her camera along when she went wig shopping with me. As I modeled one hairpiece after another, we giggled like girls playing dress-up.

I also discovered that if I could laugh about my hair loss, others could, too. My son Andrew, whose company produces special effects in the film industry, told me he didn't mind having a bald mom because he was used to seeing weird-looking aliens in movies!

Three thousand years ago Solomon said, "A cheerful heart is good medicine" (Prov. 17:22).

Dr. Dwight Carlson, whose daughter battled leukemia, witnessed this first-hand. He said, "Laughter, as well as praise and joy, not only indicates emotional health, but actually contributes to the emotional and physical healing process."[19] This is why cancer clinics now have "humor rooms" where patients can read comic books, view funny videos, or listen to humorous CDs.

Laughter and dancing go together. You will experience tremendous freedom when you give yourself permission to experience joy in your pain. It's God gift to you today.

Two Steps Back

- When was the last time you had a good laugh?
- Who do you enjoy being with the most?

Two Steps Forward

- Read Psalm 126.
- Do something today that will make you laugh. Rent a funny movie, read a humorous story, or seek out a friend with a good sense of humor.

One Step More

Dear God, thank you for giving us humor to ease the seriousness of life. Help me to see the funny side of things—and to laugh more. May my smiles be genuine. Amen.

Support Groups

Seek peace and pursue it.

Psalm 34:14

For many years I pictured support groups as gatherings of depressed misfits sharing their woes while seated on folding chairs. I decided it would never be my thing. Then I got cancer.

My first meeting for survivors of ovarian cancer was an eye-opener! I thought I had the wrong address when I drove up to a luxurious country home. Flowers and shrubs and peace were everywhere. I adjusted my wig before ringing the doorbell.

A pretty and healthy-looking middle-aged woman opened the door, hugged me, and introduced herself as Lucille. Her house was gorgeous, but I was more interested in the laughter coming from her den. This was no pity party!

I was then introduced to my ovarian cancer comrades. We sipped coffee and tea (not distilled water as I imagined!) and nibbled on cookies, fruit, and raw veggies. We told our stories. We asked questions. We laughed. We cried. There was far more optimism and resolution than tears. These were true survivors!

I came to know these women better over the next few months. We were a mixed bunch. We varied in age, size, background, religion—and hair growth. But in spite of our differences, we supported and encouraged one another. We had bonded!

I realize not all support groups are like mine. Some meet in uninteresting rooms with folding chairs. Some are not a good mix and may not meet your need. They should help you and not further depress you! After attending one for bereaved widows, a friend told me she was quitting. "All they want to talk about is how to get another husband," she told me. "I'm not into that."

You may not need a support group, but maybe somebody needs you! God provides a variety of ways to "pursue peace." This may be one. It doesn't hurt to check it out.

Two Steps Back

- Have you ever been part of a support group? If so, was it a negative or positive experience?
- Would you be willing to be part of one if you were in need of emotional or spiritual support?

Two Steps Forward

- Read Acts 2:42–47.
- If you are considering joining a support group, make some connections today. Call, write, or e-mail those agencies that handle your kind of problem.

One Step More

Dear God, thank You for all the ways You are helping me. Give me direction as to whether or not I should join a group for support right now. Amen.

Believe It

Commit everything you do to the Lord...

Psalm 37:5 (NLT)

It had been almost a year since my cancer surgery. I was in my oncologist's office for a checkup. The physical exam went well, and then he told me he would order the C125 blood test, which is the tumor marker for ovarian cancer, an indicator as to whether or not the cancer was still in remission.

"I'll order the test now, but it's up to you if you want to see the results or not. It might spoil your Christmas," he told me.

As I drove out of the clinic's parking lot, my mind was in a whirl. Did Dr. Yun know something he wasn't telling me? Had the cancer returned to haunt me once again? Fear gripped me. My chest ached and my heart pounded.

I was in a "Why me, God?" frame of mind when I passed a church. Its sign read:

Plan your future by your hopes, not your fears.

I was still thinking about that when I stopped by some friends' place to drop off a borrowed book. A rock by their front door caught my eye. On it was carved a cross and the word *BELIEVE.* I had been to their home numerous times and had never noticed that rock before!

If those two messages weren't enough, my devotional readings for that day were from Ephesians 2:10: *"For we are God's handiwork, created in Christ Jesus to do good works, which God prepared in advance for us to do."*

The devotional book's author, Amy Carmichael, wrote: *"We were created to do certain things which God thought about and*

93

*planned long before we knew anything about them... If you are
already fitted into that place, and doing the work planned for
you, then carry on with joy and without fear.*[20]

God used a sign, a stone, and a book to give me peace. And I
believe He has a variety of ways to give you His messages of
love as well. Are you looking?

Two Steps Back

- Have you tried recently to see signs of God's love and
  encouragement?
- Are you willing to look for them today?

Two Steps Forward

- If you marked Bible verses that have helped you in the
  past, read over some of them now.
- Read Ephesians 3:14–21.

One Step More

Lord, thank You for the different ways You ease my fears. I
acknowledge I need Your help today, so help me spot Your signs
of love and encouragement. Amen.

Valley Victories

May the mountains bring prosperity to the people,
the hills the fruit of righteousness.

Psalm 72:3

When Peter, James, and John followed Jesus up a mountain one day, they may have thought they were on a vacation. They had no idea their carpenter friend would be transformed into the majestic Messiah before their eyes. And they were stunned to find themselves in the company of Moses and Elijah!

Peter's reaction was quite human. He was speaking from his heart when he said, "Rabbi, it is good for us to be here." I'm sure he was shocked when a cloud came over them and a voice boomed, "This is my beloved Son. Hear *Him!*" He would have been quite happy to remain in that blissful spiritual state forever.

We all enjoy spiritual mountaintop experiences. Glimpses of Christ's power and glory are thrilling. However, it's not God's plan for us to remain above the clouds. We are needed in the valleys where real life goes on, and real people need our help.

Remember, Jesus walked down the mountain into the valley with his disciples. He didn't leave them. He knew the surreal experience was forever etched in their minds. They would need to remember Him as the transfigured Christ, the risen Lord, when their faith would later be tested.

Jesus will also take you to the heights so you will know Him better. He will then walk with you in your valleys to test your faith and to develop you into material for service to others.

Hans Christoffersen said, "It is in the humdrum and tension of daily life that we must live this hope in the paradox of putting our faith in a man who conversed with Moses and Elijah, yet died hanging helplessly on a cross."

Turn the tension in your life into a testimony. The God who revealed Himself to you in the past is still with you today.

Two Steps Back

- When was the last time you had a spiritual mountaintop experience?
- Have you ever wondered why you couldn't stay in a state of great faith?

Two Steps Forward

- Read Psalm 43.
- Write in your journal about how a mountaintop experience helped you later deal with the realities of the valley.

One Step More

Thank You, Lord, for revealing Yourself to me. Help me to remember that You are still with me in my valley. Keep me alert to Your plan and purpose. Amen.

Facing Facts

You have redeemed me,
O Lord God of truth.

Psalm 31:5 (NKJ)

Where do you go when your world seems to be shifting on the sands of uncertainty? What do you cling to when there's nothing firm in your life? For starters, you hold on to *truth*.

When Catherine Marshall lost her minister husband, Peter Marshall, through death, she felt suddenly deprived of love, strength, and financial resources. In her book *To Live Again*, she wrote:

"I did not yet know where the comfort of God's strength was leading me or what I was to do with it. Yet during those days, God was steadily asking me not to fear where Truth would lead. Truth may be painful, but it makes us free. God is not interested in coddling us, but in liberating us for further creativity, for the new life that we are forced to make."[21]

Catherine had come to terms with her husband's death. Raising their son alone, she would be facing loneliness and financial concerns. She claimed this truth, however, for herself and her son: *"And we know that all things work together for good to them that love God, to them who have been called according to his purpose"* (Romans 8:28).

This truth eventually led Catherine to publish her deceased husband's sermons in book form. She then went on to write a number of inspirational books. By facing the fact that she had a gift for writing, she carved both a living and a ministry for herself.

The coin of truth has two sides. Although you should acknowledge God's power and your personal strengths, you must also face weaknesses and shortcomings.

Two Steps Back

- In dealing with your current challenge, do you feel you were at fault in any way?
- Could you have done something differently? Do you need to ask someone for forgiveness?

Two Steps Forward

- Read John 8:31–36.
- Examine your situation carefully. Be honest. Write down what you believe to be "Truth" and "Lies."

One Step More

Lord, sometimes it's hard to face reality. Help me to be willing to accept truth today. Help me also to be truthful in all I do and say. Amen.

Relaxation Technique

He will call upon me, and I will answer him.

Psalm 91:15

Bob was taking his usual morning walk when a garbage truck pulled up beside him. He thought the driver was going to ask for directions. Instead, he showed him a picture of a cute little five-year-old boy.

"This is my grandson, Jeremiah," he said. "He's on a life-support system at the Phoenix hospital."

Thinking the man would ask for a contribution for hospital bills, Bob reached for his wallet. But the concerned grandfather wanted something else.

"I'm asking everybody I can to say a prayer for him," he continued. "Would you say one for him, please?"

Bob says he did, and that his own problems didn't seem like much that day.

When you don't know where to turn to next, you can always ask others to pray. You will relax more when you realize that you don't have to carry this burden by yourself.

When I was going through my divorce, a godly retired missionary told me she was praying for my children every day. I was greatly relieved. Whenever I began worrying about the kids, I told myself that God would certainly hear *her* prayers!

Asking others to pray is scriptural. The Bible says we are to "share each other's troubles and problems, and so obey our Lord's command" (Gal.6: 2, TLB). Christ's command is to love. Someone said, "A real friend warms you by his presence, trusts you with his secrets, and remembers you in his prayers."

99

Prayer and faith go hand in hand. That is why you need others to pray for you. They are not as near to the situation as you are, so their faith is probably in better shape than yours is at the moment.

If a garbage collector can ask a man on the street to pray, you can call or write a friend or acquaintance for backup. Sharing the load will be good for both of you. And if you find your worries are keeping you awake, remind yourself that others are probably praying while you sleep.

Two Steps Back

- Have you received help and encouragement in the past from those who were praying for you?
- Whose prayers do you think would be the most beneficial to you right now?

Two Steps Forward

- Read Colossians 3:12–17; 4:2–6.
- Contact a pastor or Christian friend and ask them to pray for a specific need.

One Step More

Dear God, thank You for the friends You have brought my way. Help me to ask for their prayers when I need it. I will sleep better knowing others are interceding for me. Amen.

A Good Prescription

But I have calmed and quieted myself,
I am like a weaned child with its mother;
like a weaned child I am content.

Psalm 131:2

Several years ago I began experiencing some unfamiliar pains. At first I tried to ignore them. But when they started robbing me of sleep, I decided to visit my doctor.

Dr. Wright examined me and asked a lot of questions. He jotted my answers down, gave me a prescription, and ordered lab work. He then told me I shouldn't worry, but it could be a life-threatening disease!

As I drove home from his office, my thoughts became as scattered as loose garbage on a windy day. Was my will in order? What would Allen do without me? How could I possibly tell the children I was dying? What would I do with my last days?

There were problems in taking some of the required tests. "I'll be dead by the time I get the tests done," I lamented to Allen. He sympathized but reminded me I could be worrying for nothing.

About that time the *Reader's Digest* came in my mail. When I opened it to "5 Ways to Conquer Worry," I had a feeling I had just been handed another prescription. The article, part of a speech given by Dr. David B. Posen, a stress-management consultant, was simple and practical. He didn't say anything I hadn't heard before, but his advice hit home.

"Remember," Dr. Posen concluded, "If something is out of your hands, worry is futile. If it *is* within your control, do something about it. Either way, worry adds nothing except more stress."[22]

Those words made sense to my analytical mind. They also reminded me of one of my favorite Bible verses: *"Don't worry about anything; instead pray about everything. Tell God what you need, and thank him for all that he has done. Then you will experience God's peace, which exceeds anything we can understand. His peace will keep your hearts and minds in Christ Jesus"* (Philippians 4:6, 7, NLT).

I made a point after that not to worry. Whenever I was tempted, I would tell myself that it was okay to be concerned (there is a difference), but I had taken the necessary tests, I was taking my medication, and the rest was up to God.

When the final test results turned out negative, I was thankful I had not wasted my time in needless worry—and unnecessary stress! The good doctor and the good Lord were both right.

Two Steps Back

- What is on your mind the most these days?
- Are you prone to worry more than you should?

Two Steps Forward

- Read Isaiah 50.
- Write out Proverbs 3:5–6 if you haven't already done so.

One Step More

Lord, please forgive me if I sometimes feel that Your hand is too short to meet my needs. Please extend your forgiveness and help today. And help me not to worry about things over which I have no control. Amen.

Light in Darkness

Are your wonders known in the place of darkness,
or your righteous deeds in the land of oblivion?

Psalm 88:12

Darkness often generates negative responses. The blackness of a night can magnify feelings of fear, hopelessness, and helplessness. Most of us feel much more in charge of our lives on a sunny day.

However, there is a bright side to a black night. It takes a clear dark evening for us to see the stars and planets that inhabit the solar systems of our universe. Even a porch light can obstruct the view of a dashing comet or the dancing of the aurora borealis.

In his book, *Powerful Prayers,* talk show host Larry King relates the story of Dr. Cecil Murray, who pastored the A.M.E. Baptist Church of Los Angeles. At that time, the church had a membership of more than two million members and seven thousand congregations throughout the world.

At age twenty-eight, Cecil had been a jet radar intercept officer for the US Air Force's Air Defense Command. One morning, while on a routine training mission in a two-seat F-89 Scorpion jet fighter, the plane's nose tank exploded on takeoff.

"I said right there, to the Lord, 'Hold me,'" Dr. Murray told King. "The Lord settled me down so I could take off the parachute and the life jacket, unbuckle the seat belt, place my head in the tiny opening in the canopy, and pull myself out."

The severely burned pilot died a month after the crash. Murray said he didn't have an answer as to why he was spared.

"There is no rational answer. There is salvation of your sanity by feeling that when life closes a door God opens a window."

Cecil Murray claims the airplane crash changed his life forever. That one dark moment in his life turned him toward Jesus Christ.[23]

There are things you will never experience, or even enjoy, unless you pass through some dark times. Compassion, empathy, and patience are all learned in the black moments of life. You may not realize the magnitude of God's love, mercy, and faithfulness until a light in your life has gone out. Facets of His divine personality you've not known will be revealed. Glimpses of His grace will be disclosed. He will shine brightest in your darkest hour.

Two Steps Back

- Have you seen some good things happen as a result of your heartache?
- Are you able to dwell on these things in the darkness of the night?

Two Steps Forward

- Read Psalm 127:1–2.
- Write in your journal some positive possibilities that may occur as a direct result of your dark night.

One Step More

Help me, God, not to fear the dark times of my life. Thank You for reminding me that the sun will shine tomorrow. Keep me safe in Your presence tonight. Amen.

Becoming Unstuck

I will instruct you and teach you in the way you should go;
I will counsel you with my loving eye on you.

Psalm 32:8

The directions said to grease the pan. I figured my non-stick cookie sheet, although old and scratched, didn't need any extra lubrication. But the instant I pulled the pizza out of the oven, I had a strong hunch it wasn't going anywhere.

Our son, Travis, then age six, took his turn to bless the food. "Dear Jesus," he prayed, "thank You for this food, bless it to our bodies, and help Mom get the pizza out of the pan. Amen."

You can bet I made an extra effort to dislodge our supper! Unfortunately, we ended up with spoonfuls of pizza instead of slices. I wondered how Travis would react to his "unanswered prayer," but I didn't have to be too concerned.

"Mom," he said, "maybe Jesus wants to teach you to grease the pan!"

Sometimes we find ourselves stuck in life because we forgot to grease our pans. Somewhere along the way we failed to follow the basic instructions for good living as laid out in the Bible. We've ignored certain commandments or warnings. The prophet Isaiah said, "We all, like sheep, have gone astray, each of us has turned to his own way" (Isaiah 53:6).

God's rules are His boundaries to keep us safe and happy. He has built into every human being a conscience that works like a high-speed computer. Even those who have never laid eyes on a Bible know when they are on the wrong side of the fence.

Fortunately, God has provided a way for us to become unstuck. It's called forgiveness. The apostle John said: *"If we claim that we're free from sin, we're only fooling ourselves... On the other hand, if we admit our sins—make a clean breast of them—he won't let us down; he'll be true to himself. He'll forgive our sins and purge us of all wrongdoing"* (1 John 1:8–9, The Message).

God's forgiveness is the spiritual oil that frees us to live the abundant life he intended us to enjoy. With our mistakes and failures behind us, we can begin anew. We can become unstuck.[24]

Two Steps Back

- Do you ever consider your behavior as direct obedience or disobedience to God?
- Do you feel you are presently living a life of obedience or disobedience?

Two Steps Forward

- Read Deuteronomy 8:6–18.
- Write in your journal: I choose to obey God today by

_____

One Step More

Dear God, You see how stuck I am today. Please forgive me for allowing myself to get in this position. Take away my sins, and free me to live the life You have planned for me. Amen.

Taking Control

You will not fear the terror of night,
nor the arrow that flies by day.

Psalm 91:5

Dr. Eric Cassell wrote in *The Healer's Art,* "If I had to pick the aspect of illness that is most destructive to the sick, I would choose the loss of control."[25]

I think this can be said of most of the "terrors" we experience in life. The death of a loved one, the loss of a job, divorce, and a great deal of other tragedies can make one feel helpless.

My mother taught me the importance of maintaining a sense of control in the face of fear. She said that when she was a girl, she often heard creaks on the stairs that led to the attic where she slept. The squeaks always stopped just behind the chimney. This gripped her with fear—until she got up the nerve to turn on the light and look behind the chimney! Upon discovering no one was hiding there, she went back to bed and slept. "When you hear a noise during the night," she said to me, "check it out."

I learned that "checking it out" was a positive way to combat my fears. If I could maintain a sense of control, I was ahead of the game. But that is sometimes easier said than done!

When my doctor told me I might have cancer, I was scared to death to "look behind the chimney." A sense of helplessness swept over me. I wasn't prepared to face the possibilities, or to tell Allen, as he had already lost one wife to illness. But his positive attitude gave me the courage to try.

I discovered there was a lot I *could* do. I could pray (difficult at first), ask others to pray (easier!), read my Bible to boost my faith, and say yes to medical treatment. I could even change my eating habits.

In his book, *When Life Isn't Fair,* Dr. Dwight Carlson states:

"...all our plans and dreams may be capsized, our bodies may be crippled, our emotions may rebel, and other people may betray us, yet still our will is free. It is free to take at least a limited amount of control in our lives, to hope for the good, to be kind to others, and to trust God amidst all the uncertainty and pain." [26]

When you are faced with a "terror by night," don't hide under the covers. Do something. Get up. Turn on a light. Pray. Check behind the chimney. Pray. Go back to sleep.

Two Steps Back

- Do you have a fear of finding out something you don't want to know?
- Do you think delaying this knowledge will help or harm your situation?

Two Steps Forward

- Read Luke 12:4–7.
- Do something today that will make you feel a bit more in control.

One Step More

Dear God, thank You for the resources You have given me. Help me to control what circumstances I can—and leave the rest with You. Amen.

Trust and Act

Trust in the Lord, and do good.

Psalm 37:3

There are two things you can concentrate on when you are going through a tough time: *trusting in the Lord* and *doing good.*

This morning I talked with a woman who is facing a major surgery. One of her main concerns is her new gynecologist's competence. I was happy to tell her that I recently had a successful operation with the same surgeon. I assured her this doctor came highly recommended from reliable sources.

Are you having problems trusting God for something? First of all, remember the millions before you who have put their confidence in Him and are happy they did. Read the Bible. Pick up a biography of a Christian giant. Talk to a pastor or priest. Go for coffee with a believer you admire. When you read about or talk with a "reliable source," your faith will be boosted. And when you experience God's power for yourself, trusting Him will be easier the next time around.

The second thing you should try is *doing good.* It's great therapy. When I was undergoing treatment for cancer, I found it helpful to phone or write someone who was also experiencing difficulties. My problems seemed minor, for instance, after listening to a friend whose son was dying of AIDS. I also found writing thank-you notes to those who were praying for me was a great distraction. When writing became difficult at one point, I tried to pray for those I knew were in need. And when praying became an effort, I rested in the fact that God knew I had good intentions!

Just for today: *Trust in the Lord and do good.* Have faith in a God who loves you, and make an effort to do something nice for someone else. A smile counts!

Two Steps Back

- Who do you admire for their level of faith?
- Why do you think their faith is so strong?

Two Steps Forward

- Pick one of my suggestions to help boost your faith. Take action!
- Do at least one good deed today. Write what you accomplished in your journal and how it made you feel.

One Step More

Dear God, please help me to give You all my doubts and fears. And lead me to someone who is in need of Your mercies. Just for today, help me to trust You and do good. Amen.

An Adventure

Though you have made me see troubles,
many and bitter,
you will restore my life again...

Psalm 71:20

I once read the incredible story of Lonnie Dupre and John Hoelscher's attempt to circumnavigate Greenland, the world's largest island, by kayak and dogsled. Although adverse conditions stopped them from completing their goal in one expedition, they covered over 11,000 miles on their first try.

The two men showed tremendous courage against all odds. Their fragile kayaks were battered by monstrous waves in the frigid waters. Huge icebergs blocked their passage. Immense ice chunks almost crushed them. They had to train ferocious and high-strung sled dogs, a slow and painstaking process. Then they faced constant peril as they ascended and descended glaciers, dodged crevices, and crossed flat fjord ice in blizzards. Frostbite, hypothermia, and hunger became familiar foes.

But in spite of all the above, Lonnie and John were determined to complete their mission. Lonnie later described the expedition as "the trip of a lifetime," and John pointed out the positives: "the colors of the twilight sky, the company of the tough and joyful Inuit, who always made us feel welcome, and the friendship with our dogs and with each other."[27]

You may never experience an adventure so ominous, but a crisis is not unlike an expedition—a test of endurance while exploring the unknown. You too can witness beauty in the sunset of even the most difficult day.

I now think of my "cancer expedition" as a valuable life experience. Up until then, I had little knowledge of, or empathy for, physical suffering. As I struggled through a major surgery, chemotherapy, radiation treatments, and hair loss, my stamina and courage sometimes surprised me. So did the times I was a wimp. I definitely got to know myself better, and my compassion for others with physical ailments increased.

But above all, I became more intimate with God. All my bravado was nothing compared to His love and faithfulness. In short, what seemed like a tragedy became the "trip of a lifetime."

Two Steps Back

- Do you think of your present problems as a journey or a bad place to land?
- Have you learned anything from this experience so far?

Two Steps Forward

- Read Psalm 95.
- Make a list in your journal of what a difficult situation you faced or are facing has taught you.

One Step More

Dear God, help me to see this trial as an expedition of faith. Give me courage and strength as I travel this journey into the unknown—with great possibilities. Amen.

Got a Petra?

Who will bring me into the strong city?
Who will lead me to Edom?

Psalm 60:9

At the time David asked these questions, the Israelites and Edomites were enemies. In order to conquer the latter, his armies would first have to find and occupy Petra, the capitol of Edom.

Naturally defended by surrounding sandstone mountains, this "strong city" could only be reached by one route, and it was a long and difficult one. David knew the first step in this particular crusade was to find the pass that led to Petra—and he needed help.

In verse 12, David answers his own question: "Through God we will do valiantly." And according to 2 Samuel 8:14, that's exactly what happened. After a successful victory, David placed garrisons throughout all Edom—"and the Lord preserved David wherever he went."

What Petra are you facing today? Have you been searching for a way to solve what seems to be an impossible problem? I suggest you look closely at how David handled his dilemma.

First of all, admit you need guidance. No matter how perplexing your situation, there is an answer. God is your best bet. He knows a way, and it will be the best one. Then, like David, think positively. You *will* be brave and courageous because God *is* going to do wonders for you.

Although the inhabitants of Petra were the enemy, the city itself, carved from red sandstone, was a wonder to behold. Keep reminding yourself that someday you will look back on your

113

passage today, and you will be able to see some beauty in it. It's God's promise to you.

Two Steps Back

- Are you facing a problem that seems unsurpassable?
- Do you believe that God can show you a way *through* this mountain?

Two Steps Forward

- Read Mark 10:23–27.
- Write these words from a song in your journal: "The Lord knows the way through the wilderness. All I have to do is follow."

One Step More

Dear God, thank You for bringing me to this place, a destination with a great purpose. Please help me to conquer my fears and doubts today, and please make what seems impossible possible. Amen.

Best Friend

I will be glad and rejoice in your love,
for you saw my affliction
and knew the anguish of my soul.

Psalm 31:7

Friendships are paramount when we face heartache. But we often keep hurt to ourselves, hiding it even from those who are close to us. Somehow we want to spare them, not to burden them. We may, on the other hand, be self-conscious and embarrassed about what has happened. Maybe we just don't know how to communicate our innermost feelings. Whatever the reason, we shut out vital help in our greatest time of need.

This verse suggests you cannot ignore the friendship God offers. Whether you like it or not, He knows every detail of your circumstance. He is fully aware of what it has done to you—and how you are reacting.

In his book, *The Purpose Driven Life*, Rick Warren warns, *"Friendships are often tested by separation and silence; you are divided by physical distance or you are unable to talk. In your friendship with God, you won't always feel him close... During times of spiritual dryness, you must patiently rely on the promises of God, not your emotions, and realize that he is taking you to a deeper level of maturity. A friendship based on emotion is shallow indeed."*[28]

Since God not only knows you but understands you, it only makes sense to respond to the help He is offering as a loving friend—whether you feel like it or not. The psalmist took the first step by stating, "I will." You too must be willing to let Him work in your life if you want to enjoy the full benefit of His friendship.

During my chemotherapy and radiation treatments, cards of encouragement would arrive in my mailbox just when I needed them most. I kept these in a metal Botticelli chocolate box, and called it my Encouragement Box. God, as your friend, has given you an Encouragement Book called the Bible. When He seems distant, just reach for an uplifting verse. He won't disappoint you; He's your Friend.

Two Steps Back

- Who are the friends that have helped you the most during this time?
- Do you feel God is your best friend?

Two Steps Forward

- Read Psalm 31:1–8.
- Write down the qualities of a good friend. Then think over this list in terms of your relationship with God.

One Step More

Dear Father, thank You for the friendship You offer me even when I don't feel Your presence. Help me to trust You in spite of my fears and failures. Amen.

A Feather Bed

He will cover you with his feathers,
and under his wings you will find refuge...

Psalm 91:4

The psalmist David was familiar with eagles from his days as a young shepherd. Not only did he watch the great birds soar with awesome grace and beauty, but he also observed their nesting habits. He no doubt was intrigued as he watched the mother eagle cover her offspring with her gigantic wings, protecting them from predators and nature's ravaging elements. Under her feathers, the eaglets were safe and warm and content.

I once lived near the ocean on Canada's Vancouver Island. I watched bald eagles fly high above the waves that lapped the rocky shoreline. I especially enjoyed observing them tend the nest in a large fir near our backyard. I noticed they were especially vigilant once their offspring were hatched. They would fly away to find food, but they were never far. One squawk from the aerie and mom would be there.

God designed eagles so that every day their bodies exude fresh oil from the inside out. This coats their feathers and weatherproofs them. Their well-equipped plumage provides the perfect shelter for their little ones.

This psalm paints a vivid picture of God's weatherproof love for you. When you do not have the strength or courage to fly on your own, you can be assured that His watchful eye will never stray from you. He will give you the warmth of His presence so that you will be filled with His peace in spite of the winds of adversity that may surround you. He has promised never to leave you nor forsake you.

He is nourishing you from His perpetual reserve of goodness. He is fully aware of every physical, mental, emotional, and spiritual need you have at this time. He has a thousand ways to supply each necessity.

God will cover you with His feathers as long as you choose to stay under His divine protection. You will fly again. You will even soar. Your strength will come from the oil of His Spirit that He will place in your wings. Whether you are too weak to leave His constant vigil or have the strength to meet the winds, you will still need to be under His watchful eye. Now that is security—and that should help you sleep!

Two Steps Back

- When in your life have you felt the most secure?
- Do you believe that God can give you the sense of security you long for?

Two Steps Forward

- Read Psalm 36:7–12.
- Write out Isaiah 26:3 and place it on your bed stand.

One Step More

Father, thank You for Your love for me and for Your constant vigil. I know I cannot fly on my own, so teach me Your ways. Amen.

Your Security

"Because he loves me," says the LORD, "I will rescue him;
I will protect him, for he acknowledges my name."

Psalm 91:14

Security is a basic human need. Every person has the built-in instinct to be free of fear and danger. In this verse God is promising safety to those who love Him.

Those who trust God to take care of them, however, sometimes feel betrayed. Why did they get sick? How come the mortgage hasn't been paid? Where was He when Mom passed away? What about the time everything was lost in a fire?

There are no easy answers to these questions. My guess is that God *does* keep us safe from most calamities most of the time. But there are occasions when He steps aside and allows something to happen in order to protect us from a larger danger.

When my friend Brenda, for example, died from cancer, I questioned God's love and timing. A lovely Christian, she had devoted her last two years to caring for her invalid husband. Wasn't God being unfair to both of them? It seemed that way at the time. I now believe, however, that God protected Brenda from an even greater sorrow, as her son was murdered a year after her death.

Several years ago a neighbor died from a terminal illness. John was a good man and was just starting to enjoy his retirement years. I recently learned that his only son committed suicide. Was John spared a greater grief? I don't know. I do know that John had accepted Jesus Christ into his life. His

119

happiness in heaven was certainly more advantageous to him than his problems here on earth!

When you love and trust God, you can be assured that He has your best interest in mind. Even when you don't feel it, He *is* protecting you. Someday you will be allowed to see He was there all the time.

Two Steps Back

- Do you think of yourself as a secure or insecure person?
- How do you feel about the idea that your sense of security should be based on your relationship with God?

Two Steps Forward

- Read Psalm 146.
- Write out Proverbs 3:5–6 in your journal.

One Step More

Lord, you know I love You. I don't always understand why You permit certain things, though. Help me to trust You—and Your perfect timing. Amen.

Worry-Free

But as for me, I trust in you.

Psalm 55:23

I will never forget the first phone call we received September 11, 2001. "Mom, do you know where Travis is? We just saw on the news that an airplane from Boston plowed into the World Trade Center in New York."

I looked at the clock. It was close to 6:30 a.m. Our married daughter who lived on Vancouver Island, B.C. was concerned about her twenty-nine-year-old brother who traveled a great deal on business. He had flown to Boston numerous times.

My husband and I quickly turned on the television and then called Travis. I sighed with relief when I heard his sleepy voice.

Like millions of others, I was glued to the television for most of the morning. After a while, however, I couldn't stand the tension. I walked at a fast pace around my neighborhood. I worked in the garden. I watched the sky for airplanes. Finally, I sought out Mildred Stamm's *Meditation Moments.*

The daily thought for September 11 was almost surreal. Although the book was written in 1967, the devotional could not have been timelier. Did God prompt Millie to write a truth He knew we would need on that particular date thirty-four years later?

The daily scripture was "Be careful for nothing," Philippians 4:6 (KJV), and the subject was worry:

"Worry exhausts the mind, depresses the spirit and wearies the body. It leaves the cares exactly as they were. Worry implies that God cannot handle our burdens... But we can be free

from every worry, every care, every anxiety. Not one is too great for God, and He is in control. Worry and trust do not go together... The secret of a life free from worry in all things is to commit them to God."[29]

Millie's words were tall orders. How could any of us not be apprehensive when thousands were dying from an atrocity too horrible to comprehend? What mother would not worry if her son were on one of those planes? Impossible!

Still, the author's words ring true. Why? Because good overcomes evil, miracles replace madness, love conquers hate. God indeed was in control on September 11, 2001. He still is today.

Two Steps Back

- What does "trust" look like to you? What makes someone trustworthy?
- Do you think God is worthy of your trust? What do you think keeps you from depending on Him more?

Two Steps Forward

- Read Isaiah 26:1–12.
- Write in your journal the name of someone you trust. Then write down the reasons you can trust them. Compare this with God's trustworthiness.

One Step More

Lord, please never let me forget that You are in charge here, not me. Help me to remember that nothing is too difficult for you—NOTHING. Amen.

Watching

The eyes of the LORD are on the righteous,
and his ears are attentive to their cry.

Psalm 34:15

During the Easter season I was explaining Christ's death and resurrection to my four-year-old granddaughter, Aydrian, while she was bathing.

"Why did Jesus go up in the sky?" she wanted to know.

"If He stayed on earth," I explained, "He could only be in one place at one time. Now He can be with each one of us all the time. We can't see Him, but He can see us."

Aydrian's big brown eyes widened. "Can He see me in the bathtub?"

Her words reminded me that God's eyes never leave us even when it makes us uncomfortable. We must never forget, however, that He always sees us through the eyes of love.

Wherever you are today, whatever challenges you are facing, God is watching. He's not waiting for you to make a mistake but rather is hoping you will make the right choices that will enhance your growth and happiness. Like a parent guarding a wobbly toddler, He stands ready to pick you up should you fall. His arms are outstretched to give you confidence to walk and run and climb. He is observing your every move because He loves you.

When friends visit with their preschoolers, they ask that a "gate" be placed at the top of the living room stairs to keep their kids safe. The blockade is for the moments when an adult may take their eyes off a child who is playing near the steps.

God doesn't need gates. When you lose your footing and start to fall, He is there to catch you. He *never* takes His eyes off you. "The eternal God is your refuge, and underneath are the everlasting arms" (Deut. 33:27). You can sleep knowing He is still on guard.

Two Steps Back

- How does it make you feel that God is watching you at all times?
- Do you think He is watching you like a doting mother or an angry father?

Two Steps Forward

- Read Deuteronomy 33:26–29.
- Write in your journal a time when you felt God was watching over you to protect you.

One Step More

Dear Father, thank You for watching over me. I now give my concerns to You. I know they are in safekeeping while I rest. Amen.

Gain in Pain

The LORD will vindicate me;
your love, LORD, endures forever—
do not abandon the works of your hands.

Psalm 138:8

Shortly after a windstorm swept through our area, our neighbor Irene took action. Fearing the large evergreen tree near her house might fall in the next gale, she had it topped. Since we can see her backyard from our kitchen window, I was disappointed with the results. The once majestic tree was now disfigured. Our neighbor felt safe, but I didn't like my new view!

As I sipped my morning coffee and looked over at Irene's funny-looking tree, I had to remind myself that beauty is not always best. Irene had peace. New growth eventually would repair the damage.

This incident reminded me how God sometimes allows us to be "topped off." In our loss and pain, we feel the beauty of life has disappeared. But He knows what He is doing. He could very well be preparing us for a greater storm. He doesn't want us to fall under the force of the next gale or the fierce attacks from Satan. And He knows that this experience will produce new growth. In the end we will once again stand tall and strong.

Shortly after my first husband asked me for a divorce, I packed my bags and headed for my sister Carolyn's home in order to get myself together. While there, I was determined to hear from God. Morning after morning I searched the scriptures for comfort and guidance.

"I am the true vine, and my Father is the gardener," I read one day. "He cuts off every branch in me that bears no fruit, while every branch that does bear fruit he prunes so that it will be even more fruitful" (John 15:1-2).

Every branch that does bear fruit he prunes. I'd read that passage many times but had never noticed those words. Maybe, just maybe, I was doing something *right* instead of something wrong! God wasn't punishing me for being a failure, but rather he was allowing me to be pruned because I *was* bearing fruit for him. It was a thought that gave me tremendous hope in my lowest moments. And pain can mean gain for you as well.

Two Steps Back

- Can you think of a time when good came from what you thought was a horrible situation?
- Can you now see God's hand in the pain you endured? Were you aware that He was with you all along?

Two Steps Forward

- Read John 15:1–17.
- Write in your journal some ideas you may have as to why you are experiencing difficulties.
  Do you think God may be pruning you for greater service?

One Step More

Dear God, I sometimes don't understand why You allow suffering. I know You love me and have a plan for my life. Please fulfill Your purpose in me. Amen.

Time to Talk

Set a guard over my mouth, LORD;
keep watch over the door of my lips.

Psalm 141:3

After the memorial service for their murdered son, Adam, a friend invited John and Revé Walsh to spend some time at a vacation home on a lake.

The friend was aware that John was "slipping away," so he made a point of almost forcing him to get up in the mornings and go for canoe rides. He also got John to talk about the tragedy:

"In the afternoons, he found me wherever I was and announced: 'I'm going to sit with you. I'm not going to pontificate, just listen.' And that's what he did. He listened to me for hours and hours and hours."[30]

Talking through your frustrations and fears is great therapy when you are dealing with a crisis. That's why therapists and psychologists do far more listening than counseling. Answers to specific problems often become apparent as you speak about them with a good listener.

There is a danger, however, of telling more than you should to the wrong person at the wrong time. Sometimes truth becomes distorted during the grieving process, and you may say things that you will regret later. And there is always the possibility of unintentionally hurting someone.

"Guarding your mouth" does not mean that you can't verbalize how you feel. It simply means to be careful with whom you speak. Don't pour out your woes to just anybody. Choose a good counselor or a trusted friend. It's much better to dump on a selected few than to let the whole world know how miserable you are. Later, when you have worked through your grief, you will have fewer regrets. You will be thankful you were tight-lipped at the appropriate time.

Two Steps Back

- Do you have a trusted friend or counselor with whom you can share your deepest thoughts and feelings right now?
- Are you willing to bear your soul to them?

Two Steps Forward

- Read Psalm 119:145–152.
- Make an appointment to talk out your fears and frustrations with someone you trust.

One Step More

Dear God, thank You for those who are willing to listen to me. Bless them, and help them to keep what I have shared in confidence. Help me to be honest with them—and with myself. Help me to "guard my mouth" when necessary. Amen.

Worth the Wait

*The LORD will indeed give what is good,
and our land will yield its harvest.*

Psalm 85:12

Our friends Gordon and Birgitta have a large Granny Smith apple tree in their front yard. I learned they planted it for their adult son's twelfth birthday.

"That was all Jason asked for his birthday," Birgitta told me. "He said he just wanted a Granny Smith apple tree, so that's what we got him!"

"And has he enjoyed the apples?" I asked.

"Oh, no, he hasn't eaten a single one. He doesn't like fruit— just like his father."

I found it a bit humorous that they gave him a gift that they knew he probably would not enjoy—just because he asked for it. And the cute little present is now a large tree that dominates their small front yard!

I believe God sometimes gives us what we ask for even though He knows it is not what we really need in the end. It may be because He enjoys giving us our desires (as our friends did for their son), or to show us it really wasn't what was good for us in the first place.

Our verse today says the Lord will give what is *good.* If we trust Him with our wants and needs, He will give us what is best. He won't give us apples when He knows we don't like fruit. Because He has created us as individuals with special talents, likes, and dislikes, He custom-makes His gifts for us.

Be careful what you ask for. I find Psalm 106:15 a bit frightening: "And he gave them their request, but sent leanness into their soul." It is better to give God permission to give us what He knows we really need.

Even when something is good for us in the end, it is better to wait for God's timing in the matter. He has so many pleasant surprises for each of us—if we only are willing to wait.

Two Steps Back

- How do you feel about waiting for God's best?
- Do you believe He loves you and truly desires what is best for you?

Two Steps Forward

- Read Psalm 85.
- Write these words in your journal or as a sign: "God gives His best to those who leave the choice with Him."

One Step More

God, help me to wait for Your best in my life. And keep me from wanting things that would only bring others and myself grief. Amen.

Running Smart

I waited patiently for the LORD;
he turned to me and heard my cry.

Psalm 40:1

Several years ago, a book I read peaked my interest in bicycle races. I followed the Tour de France, the biggest cycling race in the world, on television and in the newspapers. I was especially intrigued by the strength and endurance of the cyclists.

I learned that pacing oneself is important in cycle racing as it is in many other athletic competitions. "Riding smart" is extremely difficult for those who are accustomed to pushing themselves to the limit one hundred per cent of the time.

"I still struggled with impatience at times," one rider explained. "I would ride smart for a while, and then backslide. I just couldn't seem to get it through my head that in order to win I had to ride more slowly at first. It took some time to reconcile myself to the notion that being patient was different from being weak, and that racing strategically didn't mean giving less than all I had."[31]

After crashing twice, it took a lot of self-control for the cyclist to hold back. But he "waited and waited" until just the right moment to make his move—on a steep ascent. He raced ahead of the others up the incline and then down the other side, a long and dangerous slope. But his patience paid off; he had enough strength to win.

The apostle Paul wrote: *"Do you not know that in a race all the runners run, but only one gets the prize? Run in such a way to get the prize. Everyone who competes in the game goes into strict training. They do it to get a crown that will not last; but we do it to get a crown that will last forever. Therefore I do not run like a man running aimlessly"* (1 Cor. 9:24–26).

The life of a Christian is a discipline. Often what we think is unfair or unnecessary is in reality God's way of training us to be winners for His glory. His ways and timing are always perfect. He is pacing us for the big finish. Persevere and some day you will be presented to the King of Kings—a winner.

Two Steps Back

- Have you thought that the problems you are facing today may be God's way of slowing you down for a better "finish?"
- Are you willing to "pace yourself" so that God can use you in a greater way someday?

Two Steps Forward

- Read 1 Corinthians 9:19–27.
- Make a timeline of the big events in your life. Can you see how minor actions have determined major outcomes? Can you see a pattern? What do you think you can do to promote more positive results in the future?

One Step More

Dear God, thank You for the special race You have designed for me. Help me to remember that waiting can very well be Your way of pacing me for the big win. Amen.

Worth the Risk

The voice of the LORD is over the waters;
the God of glory thunders,
the LORD thunders over the mighty waters.

Psalm 29:3

Years ago I dined on a ship that had been converted into a restaurant. After being seated in captain chairs, my companion and I were served a variety of seafood. We thoroughly enjoyed the food and nautical atmosphere, but there was one thing missing: The boat wasn't going anywhere. It had been built to navigate the ocean—not to be moored in a harbor as a dining room!

I once saw a poster of a peaceful scene of a ship leaving a picturesque harbor to venture into the open sea. The caption read: "A ship in a harbor is safe, but this is not what ships are built for."

When the storms of life get rough, it's tempting to find a quiet port and anchor. That's okay as long as you remember you can't stay there forever. There comes a time when you have to hit the high seas again. God has a destination in mind for you. You will face some more strong gales. There will be risks. But He has promised never to abandon you.

In his book, *A Gift of Hope: How We Survive Our Tragedies,* Dr. Robert Veninga wrote: "Probably the most difficult part of the journey in recovering from a heartbreak is to take risks. To actually believe that you can find a new job, a new way of life. And it is particularly difficult to take risks if you have convinced yourself that your situation will never change."[32]

133

Doug Anakin, the risk-taker who won a gold medal for bobsledding in the 1964 Olympics said, "You have to stand on two feet. One is risk. One is security."[33]

As you venture out again into whatever life has in store for you, remember fear is your worst enemy. Keep focused on your destination and not on the winds of doubt or the dark clouds of failure. Welcome risks and you will witness God standing at your helm. You will hear His voice "over the waters"—and you will know true security.

Two Steps Back

- How do you feel about taking risks? What is the biggest risk you've ever taken?
- Are you willing to take a risk in your present situation? Do you believe God will help you?

Two Steps Forward

- Read Matthew 14:22–36.
- Determine to do something you believe God wants you to do even though it is out of your comfort zone. Write your intentions in your journal and take a step in that direction.

One Step More

Lord, sometimes I don't think I can face another storm. Calm my fears and keep me focused on You. If a risk is involved, help me. Amen.

Your Inheritance

He chose our inheritance for us,
the pride of Jacob, whom he loved.

Psalm 47:4

During a speaking tour, I stayed in the home of a semi-retired lawyer and his wife. I admired their large, elegant home with its fine furnishings and tasteful artwork. I was more impressed, however, with the woman's attitude regarding the future of their estate.

While many older people today laugh and agree with the sticker that reads, "We're spending our children's inheritance," Mabel mentioned more than once that she wanted her children to benefit financially from her passing. She had no plans to spend all their inheritance!

It's comforting to know that our heavenly Father has chosen an inheritance for us. He not only provides for our daily needs, He meets those requirements on an individual basis. He knows what is best for each of us.

Whenever you're tempted to feel sorry for yourself because others seem to be more blessed, remember that by trusting Christ you have exactly what He wants you to have—and it is His best for you. Just as parents don't *have* to leave their children anything, God doesn't owe you anything. But He has *chosen* to give you all that you need simply because He loves you.

Our verse today reads, "He chose our inheritance for us, the pride of Jacob, whom he loved." Jacob certainly wasn't a perfect person. As the ancient story goes, he tricked his twin brother into giving him the family birthright, or inheritance. Yet God changed his name to Israel, and used his offspring to bring Christ into this world.

You may feel like a failure today. Remember that God can even use your mistakes to work out a great plan. He has chosen a special inheritance just for you!

Two Steps Back

- What picture comes to your mind when you think of God as your Father?
- Has your relationship (or lack of one) with your earthly father shaped this image in any way?

Two Steps Forward

- Read Matthew 6:5–15.
- Write out the "Lord's Prayer" in your own words.

One Step More

Lord, thank You for making me Your child, and for loving me. Help me to use the inheritance You have chosen for me to bless others. Amen.

Snuggle Up

But as for me, it is good to be near God.
I have made the Sovereign LORD my refuge;
I will tell of all your deeds.

Psalm 73:28

On November 17, 2001, Allen set our bedside clock's alarm for 1:30 a.m. We didn't want to miss the Leonid meteor storm, the most spectacular meteor shower of the century.

Every November, the earth passes through hundreds of thousands of meteorites left in the wake of the comet Tempel-Tuttle when the sun's heat rends its frozen surface. Normally, under the right conditions, about ten meteors per hour can be spotted during one of these showers. But in 2001 the earth passed through "debris belts" left by the comet in 1767. Those watching under clear and dark skies could see meteors shooting across the sky at the rate of one to two thousand per hour. The higher the observer's elevation, and the farther from city lights, the better the view.

We stretched ourselves out in a sleeping bag on our frosty sun deck. Although mesmerized by the fiery streaks across the sky, we were somewhat disappointed. After an hour we counted only twenty-five or so meteors—not the hundreds we anticipated.

Were the astronomers wrong? Did we doubt the news reports later that morning because others witnessed more meteors? Certainly not. We just happened to live close to sea level and where streetlights hampered a good view of the meteor storm.

In a similar way, why question the love and power of God simply because you can't see it at the moment? The reports are all in. He *is* working on your behalf right now. You just need to position yourself closer to Him.

Just as a meteor storm is best seen in darkness, God often shines brightest in your blackest night. Your moments of despair position you to witness His mercy, love, and forgiveness. As you draw closer to Him through prayer, Bible reading, and fellowship with Christians, you will witness His goodness—and it's pretty spectacular!

Two Steps Back

- When have you felt God the closest to you?
- Do you sense He is near or far away right now?

Two Steps Forward

- Read Job 23:8–17.
- For a week, keep a record of those moments when you feel God is close or working on your behalf.

One Step More

Dear Lord, I don't always see how You are working. Forgive me for doubting Your love and forgiveness. Help me to draw closer to You and to know You better. Amen.

Be Courageous!

Be strong and take heart,
all you who hope in the LORD.

Psalm 31:24

When Air Canada went into bankruptcy, thousands of the company's employees were laid off. One of those workers was Harry, a structure technician. His wife Melody and I were directors for an interdenominational ministry, and she asked our board to pray. Month after month, Harry searched for work. Friends and family and churches prayed. God seemed to have gone deaf. Finally, I received the following e-mail:

After 9 long challenging, stretching and faith walking months, a door spontaneously opened 2 weeks ago at a local plant propagation company… We really don't know where we would be without the tangible overwhelming support of friends and our church community. This has been the most humbling chapter of our lives. And it would be foolish to tell you that we are OK and right back to where we were a year ago. Not. The swirling doubts that stormed over and around us, the fear of financial failure, sinking and loss were very real and titanic at times. The waters have calmed for a while, but we are not letting go of the precious little life raft we've clung to—FAITH. Many a time we prayed, "God I believe, but help my unbelief!" At times we still have the swirling (yes kinda heaving stomach feeling) from being shipwrecked, drifting in the open waters without guideposts or even large landmass in sight. For now, the sky is blue and there is work. Work is so much more than a word—it brings more purpose, value, esteem and worth to one's being... and there really is nothing more desirous than to have work, labor fit to the heart and soul of who God designed us to be."³⁴

Melody and Harry's observations were right on. First, waiting is not easy. It will stretch your faith until you wonder if you have any left to stretch. Secondly, God hears our prayers. The answer may not be what we expect, but it will come. Thirdly, tested faith produces stronger faith.

Melody ended her e-mail by stating:

"As we walk these deep waters, we choose to keep looking up at Jesus lest we sink. Please continue to pray that we might be found faithful on this journey and that God might redeem the months lost, the hopes that have been set aside to do immeasurably more than we could have ever imagined."

Waiting will test your faith like nothing else. It will demand courage and determination and stamina—and love. Your love for God will keep you afloat until He sends angels your way.

Two Steps Back

- What the hardest thing you've experienced about waiting?
- In these troubled waters, are you depending on Christ to keep you afloat?

Two Steps Forward

- Read Lamentations 3:25–33.
- Highlight Lamentations 3:25 in your Bible. Then write it out in your journal—and make sure it's dated!

One Step More

Dear Lord, You alone know how long I must wait for this to pass. I do believe, but help my unbelief! Amen.

Tiny Things

All my longings lie open before you, Lord;
my sighing is not hidden from you.

Psalm 38:9

It's the small things Allen does for me that make me feel special. He often turns the covers down on my side of the bed at bedtime. In the mornings, he sometimes turns off the alarm so I can sleep an extra ten minutes, and then heats my mug with hot water to keep my coffee warm.

Oswald Chambers said, "The things that make God dear to us are not as much His blessing as the tiny things; because they show His amazing intimacy with us; He knows every detail of our individual lives."[35]

I was extremely grateful for God's protection and care after a major surgery on New Year's Eve. His love for me became even more evident by the little things that happened afterwards. For instance, as the family gathered at midnight to wish me a happy New Year, the sky outside my hospital window lit up. None of us knew we would be the spectators of an awesome fireworks display taking place in a nearby park. And I had the best "seat" in the house (or hospital!).

As I watched the bursts of color shooting high in the dark night, raining down in brilliant patterns, I felt especially close to God. He knew my disappointment when our holiday celebration plans were cancelled due to my operation, so He arranged a party. Nothing could be better than family and fireworks together after an extremely tough day!

The psalmist said God is aware of *all* our desires. Not only will He provide for our needs in the big trials of life, He will meet the small longings as well. He knows each one of us inside and out. He knows *you*. He is aware of what makes you happy—and He loves to see you smile. When you least expect it, He will arrange some fireworks just for you. It may come in the form of a letter, e-mail, something special on sale, a book by your favorite author. Keep alert. He's trying to say, "I love you."

Two Steps Back

- What are some of the small things in your life that have given you much joy?
- Do you ever think of these things or experiences as coming from God's hand?

Two Steps Forward

- Read Psalm 138.
- At the end of today, write in your journal all the small things for which you can thank God.

One Step More

Lord, thank You for all You do to make me feel special. Make me aware of Your presence in the small delights You bring my way. They tell me You know me so well, and I love You for that. Amen.

Passing It On

*Let each generation tell its children
of your mighty acts.*

Psalm 145:4 (NLT)

Normally I don't read the obituaries in the newspaper unless they are about someone I know. But one in particular caught my attention this morning. Right in the middle of the birth and death announcements was the picture of an attractive older woman named Dorothy. Underneath was the longest obituary I have ever seen—and one of the best.

Obviously written by one of Dorothy's children, it was a tremendous tribute to someone who had lived a selfless and full life. I was especially touched when I read:

"Mom was the most wonderful gift we could have ever received. She was always encouraging, guiding, loving, and giving hope. She did her best to live her life like Jesus. She always placed her family and many others before herself. As our matriarch she led us with much compassion, wisdom, and thoughtfulness. She was always there for us whenever she could be...We will truly miss her warm wonderful smile, generous affection, delicious Sunday family roast beef dinners with Yorkshire pudding; taking us to church; attending almost every school function and music recital; celebrating everyone's birthday and every festive occasion; or just taking time and sitting down and talking with us over a hot pot of tea. Mom generously volunteered and selflessly gave of her time and energy for many, and the work of the church... Mom is a part of us and will always be with us..."[36]

143

Every life has its ups and downs. Tragedy happens to us all. It's how we react to our circumstances that will leave a lasting impression. Dorothy never stopped being a shining light for her Lord. During the last year of her life she "courageously endured the debilitating effects of brain cancer." Even in the last difficult moments of her life she remained constant in her faith and selflessness.

I got the impression that Dorothy did her part in introducing the next generation to God by the way she lived. I would love to have my family put *"She did her best to live her life like Jesus"* on my tombstone! We may not have all the answers as to why we are enduring certain difficulties, but we can use our circumstances to demonstrate Christ to others—especially to our families.

Two Steps Back

- How would you like to be remembered?
- What steps can you take to influence your family and friends in a positive way?

Two Steps Forward

- Read James 1:19–27.
- Write in your journal a short summation of your life. Are you proud of your achievements or disappointed?

One Step More

Dear Lord, You know I'm not perfect, but help me to live as You did. Give me Your grace through this difficult time so that the next generation will know You are very much alive. Amen.

Reasons

For you have delivered me from death
and my feet from stumbling,
that I may walk before God
in the light of life.

Psalm 56:13

In his book, *When Life Isn't Fair*, Dr. Dwight Carlson wrote, "When we suffer, the single most important ingredient is seeing purpose in it. Lack of purpose breeds hopelessness; purpose imparts the strength to sustain."[37]

Charles and Myrtle are the kind of couple that stand out in their church and community. Leaders in a number of spiritual and social causes, they are generous with both their time and money. You would never guess they ever had to find a purpose for heartache.

Myrtle was once part of my small group in our church's Saturday morning Bible studies. We were discussing Jacob's stairway-to-heaven dream, when I asked if someone had encountered God in an unusual way. Myrtle told us about losing a seven-year-old son to a rare cancer.

"When Charlie and I lost our son, we both had this big black hole inside us. As the years went by, the hole got smaller, but it was always there. A number of years passed, something like ten or fifteen, and then I had this dream. I wasn't awake, but it was so real. I saw our son, and he said, 'It's okay, Mommy, I'm happy here.' After that experience, the hole healed much faster."

It's interesting to note that Myrtle had to wait a number of years before true restoration took place. Was God being unfair, unkind? I don't believe so. Looking at her depth of faith and commitment to Christ, I'm sure God used those empty years to fill the void with Himself—and to prepare her and Charles for Christian service.

Viktor Frankl, a Viennese psychiatrist, wrote about his five years in Auschwitz. He said, "Suffering ceases to be suffering in some way at the moment it finds a meaning."[38]

Waiting to heal—or to be happy again—is a form of suffering. It will be easier for you to accept once you realize that there is a specific purpose—not just for the pain, but for the wait as well. It will all come together in *His* time.

Two Steps Back

- How you do you feel about the idea that waiting is a form of suffering?
- Could you accept this waiting period better if you knew for certain there was a good reason for it?

Two Steps Forward

- Read Isaiah 30:18–21.
- Write in your journal some possible reasons why you must wait.

One Step More

Lord, thank You that You do not ask us to suffer needlessly. I may not understand Your purpose, but please give me Your peace. Amen.

Grow While Waiting

The righteous will flourish like a palm tree,
they will grow like a cedar of Lebanon.

Psalm 92:12

The cedars of Lebanon are incredible. Even at high elevations they grow from sixty to one-hundred feet tall. They are especially noted for their durability. Through the ages they have been used to build palaces, ships, temples, and tombs.

This psalm tells us that if we put our faith and trust in God, we can grow spiritually in such a way that we can rise above our circumstances. In so doing, we can influence generations to come. Temples and tombs last a long time!

The great Bible teacher Oswald Chambers wrote: *"If you are going to be used by God, He will take you through a multitude of experiences that are not meant for you at all, they are meant to make you useful in His hands..."*[39]

Grown chiefly in groves, over a thousand cedar trees may be found in one stand. Just as a forest can withstand a storm far better than a lone tree, so are we stronger when we have the prayers and support of fellow believers. Christian friends, a Bible-believing church, Bible studies, and prayer groups can all contribute to our spiritual growth.

It's also interesting to note that the reddish-brown wood of Lebanon's cedars is attractive, fragrant, and light. If we are truly rooted in Christ and growing strong for His purposes, His scent within us will attract unbelievers. We should be hearing, "There's something different about you..."—in a positive way, of course!

147

Are you growing like a cedar of Lebanon? Will your life live on after you are gone? The apostle Paul, who endured a great deal for his faith in Christ, wrote, "I have fought the good fight, I have finished the race, I have kept the faith" (2 Tim. 4:7). Will you be able to say that?

Two Steps Back

- Do you feel you are shrinking or growing spiritually right now?
- Are you willing to view this time of "waiting" as a period for spiritual growth?

Two Steps Forward

- Read Psalm 92:12–15.
- Ask a Christian friend or mentor (someone who knows you well) if they have seen a positive change in you since this trial began. Discuss the possibilities of spiritual growth as a result of difficult circumstances.

One Step More

Lord, thank You that you have a great purpose for my life. Help me not to be afraid of the elevations You are calling me to. As I grow strong in You, help my life to endure beyond this one. Amen.

Unfair

With words of hatred they surround me;
they attack me without cause.
In return for my friendship they accuse me,
but I am a man of prayer.

Psalm 109:3–4

Whitney was the last person I thought would end up as a divorce statistic. As a teenager, she was the blond and blue-eyed envy of the girls. Not only did she turn guys' heads, but she was also intelligent, talented, and witty—and a committed Christian.

I guess that's why I was stunned to learn her twenty-year marriage was in serious difficulty. I had never met her husband, but I assumed they were very happy together.

A letter from Whitney, however, described a relationship that was "trouble from the beginning"—affairs, verbal and emotional abuse, manipulation, bankruptcy. She said she felt she didn't deserve the hell she had been through.

Unfair? No doubt. Even Jesus indicated that life isn't always as it should be. He told His disciples that God "causes his sun to rise on the evil and the good, and sends rain on the righteous and the unrighteous" (Matt. 5:45).

You cannot use your problems as a thermometer to test your goodness. While living an honest and morally good life has its definite rewards, it is no guarantee against heartache. The "I guess I've been living right" theory simply does not apply at all times.

The employee of the month can be unemployed by the next month. Good parents have children on drugs. Great spouses lose mates to divorce or death. Wonderful people die in earthquakes, hurricanes, tornadoes, fires, and floods every year. As someone said, "Life in a fallen world seldom rewards right living."

The psalmist David, who had his share of disasters, put it in perspective when he wrote, "but I am a man of prayer." He knew God could make sense out of what seemed senseless, could create beauty out of chaos.

Fortunately, my friend Whitney was a woman of prayer. At the end of her letter she wrote, "I don't want to miss God's intention for my life... Anytime we get to prove God in a powerful way, it has its benefits!" Looking at her life today, several years later, she has proved that life may be unfair, but God remains faithful.

Two Steps Back

- Do you feel that you have been treated unfairly?
- Are you willing to allow God to bring good out of what may seem to you like a horrible injustice?

Two Steps Forward

- Read Psalm 109:22–31.
- Write a thank-you letter to God.

One Step More

Dear God, in all the unfairness of life, help me to look at it from Your perspective. Please make me a person who prays. Amen.

Keeping Focused

You make known to me the path of life;
you will fill me with joy in your presence,
with eternal pleasures at your right hand.

Psalm 16:11

There is incredible power in being focused. Sunlight, when focused on a magnifying glass, can start a fire. Laser beams, which are intensely focused light, can cut through steel. And people who direct their energies toward a focal point can accomplish a great deal in one short life.

When you are dealt a sudden blow, it's easy to forget your "path of life." It's difficult to focus on anything but the problem at hand. But having a *life focus* will motivate you to keep your present troubles in perspective—and to get on with living.

Susan Wesley (1669–1742) was a woman who knew the meaning of being focused. Her mission statement was simple: to serve God to the best of her ability and to train her children to love God.

In order to reach these objectives, Susan spent two hours daily in prayer and Bible reading. She held Christian services in her kitchen—and sometimes in her barn. She homeschooled her children daily for twenty years, and spent time with them individually.

The wife of a poor curate, she was familiar with hardship. Nine of her nineteen children died before they reached adulthood. Disease and fires plagued her family. Her husband was even jailed once. But through it all she kept focused.

Susan's determination paid off. Her son John became the founder of the Methodist church, and her son Charles wrote three thousand hymns. Her "path of life" still blesses the Christian community today!

God does not have special plans just for certain people. There is a unique design for every life—including yours. You have certain talents and abilities that He wants to use for His purposes.

First of all, His plan is to have a personal relationship with you. If you have not surrendered your life to Jesus Christ, you will have a hard time finding your life focus.

Secondly, He has special work for you. Your job may be to raise your children to be Christians, to be an encourager to others, to excel at loving your neighbors.

Think of your trials as either contributors or hindrances to your life focus. And then ask God to help you deal with them accordingly.

Two Steps Back

- What do you believe are the special talents and abilities given to you by God?
- As a child, what did you want to be when you grew up?

Two Steps Forward

- Read Psalm 16.
- Write out your mission statement.

One Step More

Dear God, forgive me for allowing my problems to overwhelm me. Help me to focus on the big picture—Your plan for my life. Help me see my present heartache as something You can use to keep me on track. Amen.

Angels

For he will command his angels concerning you
to guard you in all your ways.

Psalm 91:11

Angels are real. These ministering creatures of God are magnificent and mighty. Mainly invisible to us, they can appear as ordinary people, ghostly figures, or their majestic selves. The writer of Hebrews said they are "sent to serve those who will inherit salvation" (Hebrews 1:14).

Angels guarded the Garden of Eden, selected Isaac's wife, fought battles for Israel, shut the lions' mouths for Daniel, nourished prophets, announced Christ's birth, fed Him in the wilderness, guarded His tomb, announced His resurrection, and freed His disciples from prison. The list goes on and on.

My first possible encounter with angels was in 1968. I was a college student and my fiancé was a soldier in Vietnam. When he received a Rest and Recuperation leave to Hawaii, I desperately wanted to meet him. My parents agreed—provided my mother went with me!

Upon arriving in Hawaii, we hailed an airport limo to transport us to our hotel. A tall, good-looking man dressed in a dark suit got in with us. When he heard of our destination, he said, "You don't want to go there. I have a reservation I don't need at the ...., and I suggest you take it. Here is my name and room number."

We accepted the information and got out at the hotel he recommended. The room was exactly what we needed at the same price as our first choice. Later we checked out the first hotel. It was in the city's low-rent district, and certainly didn't appear safe.

When we prepared to leave for the airport a week later, we discovered our rented car had been stolen. If my fiancé missed his flight, he would be AWOL. Once again a stranger in a dark suit seemed to appear out of nowhere. He told us to leave the details with the hotel's security and take his taxi to the airport. We made it just in time. An angel? We would like to think so! But in any case, God was taking care of us.

God has assigned angels to protect and guide you. You can rest in peace knowing they are listening for His commands concerning you.

Two Steps Back

- Do you believe angels really exist?
- Have you ever encountered someone whom you thought could be a guardian angel?

Two Steps Forward

- Read Daniel 10.
- Write down the "angels" who have rescued you at some point. Remember, God probably sent them, whether they were celestial beings or earthlings.

One Step More

Thank you, Lord, for the angels You have assigned to protect and direct me. Forgive me for dwelling on my fears. Amen.

Listening

*Let the morning bring me word of your unfailing love,
for I have put my trust in you. Show me the way I should go,
for to you I entrust my life.*

Psalm 143:8

I have stayed in Ed and Beth's home more than once while speaking on Vancouver Island. This beautiful Christian couple has a gift for hospitality. I have especially enjoyed the guest room, with its soft pastels, tasteful decor, and comfy bed. The best feature for me, however, was the bookshelf. Put me in a room with a collection of Christian inspirational books, and you've got a permanent lodger!

"We bought a lot of those books after our son died," Beth explained to me. Their son, who had a deep Christian faith, passed away at the age of twenty-one from a serious illness. As the couple struggled with their sorrow—and questions—they read book after book on subjects like the sovereignty of God, His love, His will. They wanted to know what He was trying to tell them through what seemed like a senseless tragedy.

Beth never told me what God told them. But I do know it changed their lives forever. There is a spiritual depth to both of them, the kind that belongs to those who have passed through deep waters.

Oswald Chambers wrote: *"The goal of my spiritual life is such close identification with Jesus Christ that I will always hear God and know God always hears me... What hinders me from hearing is my attention to other things. It is not that I don't want to hear God, but I am not devoted in the right areas of my life."*[40]

Unfortunately, most of us are so preoccupied with "other things" that we aren't aware that God may be trying to say something. So often it's not until something bad happens that we are ready to listen.

Two Steps Back

- Take a hard look at your life today. Is there something God is trying to tell you?
- Are you ready to hear what He has to say?

Two Steps Forward

- Read Psalm 73:21–28.
- Keep a record of what you think God is telling you to do.

One Step More

Lord, You've got my attention. I don't understand what is happening right now, but I trust You. What are You trying to tell me through this? Please show me the way that I should go. Amen.

Waiting

*Wait for the LORD;
be strong and take heart
and wait for the LORD.*

Psalm 27:14

Allen's motto could be "I'd rather be late than wait." My sister Carolyn's could be "I'd rather knit than just sit." These two are workaholics with A-type personalities. Patiently waiting in an idle position is not one of their virtues! But *most* of us find waiting for difficult circumstances to change tough.

According to *Strong's Exhaustive Concordance of the Bible,* the word "wait"—or forms of it—appears 159 times in the King James Bible, twenty-three in the Psalms alone. (The author, Dr. James Strong, knew something about patient endurance; it took him thirty-five years to prepare the most complete concordance of the Bible's King James Version!)

Over and over we are told to "wait for the Lord"—especially when disaster strikes. Job, the man who lost his family, possessions, and health all in one swoop, said, "I will wait for my renewal to come" (Job 14:14). David was in physical pain when he wrote Psalm 69. Although he was "worn out from calling for help," he was convinced "the Lord hears the needy." The prophet Isaiah promised the depressed Israelites, "They that wait upon the Lord shall renew their strength" (Isaiah 40:31).

It's not easy to wait for better things to come. There's not much pleasure in enduring a long illness, searching for a job, watching our children make wrong decisions, aching for a loving relationship, and so on. But God quite often asks us to hang on and trust Him with these things. And He always has a good reason.

Are you waiting for Him to do something for you today? If so, you are in a good position! By not rushing ahead of God, you are strengthening your faith in His faithfulness and goodness.

But don't be idle. Imitate my husband and sister. Keep yourself occupied while you're at a standstill. Pray. Read your Bible. Do something good for someone else. Before you know it, the answer to your problem will come. God will see to it.

Two Steps Back

- Do you find waiting difficult at the best of times?
- Are you waiting for something to happen today?

Two Steps Forward

- Read Psalm 27:11-14
- Make a list of positive things you can do while you are waiting.

One Step More

Lord, You know how hard waiting is for me right now. Please quiet my anxious spirit and give me patience until your best solution arrives. Amen.

Contentment

I will extol the LORD at all times;
his praise will always be on my lips.

Psalm 34:1

Remember the Biblical account of David and Goliath? Well, Saul, the king of Israel, brought David on staff as a reward for saving his country. The young shepherd was made the commander of the troops in short order—an overwhelming assignment for a rookie!

David was an instant success. So much so that when the Israeli army returned home victorious, the women danced and sang, "Saul has slain his thousands, and David his ten thousands!"

Needless to say, this did not sit well with the king. In a jealous rage, he set out to murder David. When throwing spears at the young officer didn't work (David was a good dodger!), Saul demoted David to the rank of captain just to get him out of his sight. But David kept winning battles—and the hearts of the Israelites.

Saul's fury forced David to flee for his life. At one point, he sought asylum in Gath, a Philistine city. But the king there saw the Israelite captain as a threat to the country's security. In order to save himself, David pretended to be insane by scratching on doors and letting saliva run down his beard. When the king dismissed him as a madman, David escaped to a cave—where it is believed he wrote those famous words, "I will bless the Lord at all times."

Someone has said, "Happiness is in the heart, not in the circumstances." David obviously knew the secret of contentment. His one-on-one relationship with God had taught him the love and power of his Creator. Even as a young man, he had witnessed God's faithfulness over and over. He could live in a cave or a palace as long as God was with him.

The apostle Paul, another giant of faith, wrote: "I have *learned* the secret of being content in every situation" (Phil. 4:12, TLB). Like David, he knew his attitude could hinder his spiritual altitude.

You may need to ask God to help you learn how to be content in spite of your circumstances. The result could be life changing!

Two Steps Back

- Can you praise God even when you don't have answers?
- Are you able to thank Him for His goodness when life isn't so good?

Two Steps Forward

- Read Philippians 4:10–20.
- Make a list of the good things that have come your way recently.

One Step More

Dear God, help me to change my attitude so that my altitude in You can increase. Give me the courage and faith to trust You when I don't have the answers. Amen.

Desires

Take delight in the LORD,
and he will give you the desires of your heart.

Psalm 37:4

"I'm big enough to go to Disneyland when I'm four feet tall," Aydrian, my five-year-old granddaughter informed me. "When Breyann and Justyn are four feet tall, we can all go!"

Aydrian proudly showed me some marks on her kitchen doorway. The date and height of each child in her family were neatly printed on the wall. The mark that represented four feet had the word "Disneyland" written beside it.

Aydrian was thirteen when she and her family finally flew from Canada to Los Angeles. My daughter and her husband were wise to wait until each child was the required height for the amusement park's rides. It made their dream vacation more enjoyable—and safer!

You can't hide your longings from God. Even when you are hurting too badly to pray, He is still aware of your deepest yearnings. He hears your sighs—and sobs—when you can't verbalize how you feel or what you want.

As your heavenly Father, He would love to grant you your heart's desires, to escort you to all the "Disneylands" you've dreamed about. But He loves you too much to give you always what you want when you want it. He wants to wait until you are ready. His timing is always perfect.

Rest in the fact that He knows your heart's desires. He *wants* to see you happy. For those reasons, He will choose just the right moment to take you on an incredible journey—one you will be glad you waited for!

Two Steps Back

- What do you think is your deepest desire today?
- Do you feel it is worth waiting for—no matter how long it takes?

Two Steps Forward

- Read Psalm 116.
- Get feedback from a trusted Christian mentor as to the possible reasons your greatest desire has not been fulfilled.

One Step More

Lord, forgive my impatience. Help me to realize that my dreams are only a shadow of what You have planned for me. Help me to wait patiently for whatever that may be. Amen.

A Banner

You have given a banner...
that it may be displayed.

Psalm 60:4 (NKJ)

As the king of Israel, David often led his soldiers to war. He knew the importance of the banner, the flag raised in battle to indicate the rallying point for his men. It gave them a point of reference and encouragement. As long as the banner was visible, they were still in the game.

Those of us who enlist in the service of Jesus Christ are given a banner with His insignia of faith, hope, and love painted in brilliant colors. It should be held high for others to see as we follow Him into the spiritual warfare of life. He did not promise it would be easy.

Years ago, Isobel Kuhn, a missionary to China and Thailand, wrote a book entitled *Green Leaf in Drought-Time.* It's the story of Arthur and Wilda Mathews, who, with their little girl, were among the last of the China Inland Mission to leave China when it first succumbed to Communism.

For two years this family was kept housebound in north China by the Red Regime, which deliberately tried to starve them. They were not allowed to have any contact with Chinese Christians, which, as missionaries, was a source of frustration.

The Mathews, however, became a banner for the persecuted Christians to watch. Their lives were living examples of how to trust Jesus in the hardest of times. Often on the edge of starvation, they kept their faith strong, their hope and love intact. This was only possible because of "an unseen Source of secret nourishment, which the communists could not find and from which they could not cut them off."[41]

David became a great warrior for both God and his country because he learned early in life "the battle is the Lord's" (I Samuel 17:47). In other words, he knew the Source for victory personally.

The God of David—and the Mathews—is the same God who wants to enable you to hold His banner high in spite of your trials. He has given you the privilege of being His display of courage, faith, love—and hope.

Two Steps Back

- How do you feel about the idea of being "on display?"
- Do you feel your conduct at this time is a "banner" for Christ that your family and friends can follow?

Two Steps Forward

- Read Psalm 60.
- Ask a close Christian friend or family member if they feel you are displaying a Christ-like attitude at this time. Be determined to learn and grow from their comments.

One Step More

Dear Lord, please give me the courage to be Your banner of love and faith to those around me. Be my source of comfort and hope today. Amen.

Balance

My feet stand on level ground;
in the great congregation I will praise the LORD.

Psalm 26:12

As a child, teeter-tottering with my older sister Carolyn was always a challenge. For one thing, she outweighed me and thought it was great fun to keep me suspended in the air. My only defense was to bounce on my end of the board.

Sometimes, however, we cooperated so the weight was distributed evenly. I would scoot back as far as I dared, and Carolyn would move forward. We sat perfectly still, looking each other straight in the eye. Balance and peace—for three glorious seconds!

Life is like a teeter-totter. It can be a lot of fun—or it can become lopsided by too much weight on one end. We become frustrated when we find ourselves sitting on the ground—going nowhere fast—or up in the air, feeling useless and out of control. Either scenario causes us to lose both rhythm and balance.

Is it possible to maintain balance in your life when you become weighted down by an unforeseen heartache? While you are waiting for things to change? Can you truly have peace under such circumstances?

I believe the secret can be found in the words of a song recorded in the Bible: *"You (God) will keep him in perfect peace, whose mind is stayed on You, because he trusts in You"* (Isaiah 26:3, NKJ).

Life will remain unbalanced as long as your problems have your full attention. The best way to make your "feet stand on level ground" is to keep focused on God. You do this through prayer, reading the Bible and Christian literature, keeping alert to the voice of the Holy Spirit in your mind.

But you must do more than just *think* about God; you must *trust* Him. You must put your problems in His hands—and leave them there. And then, as my sister and I did on the teeter-totter, *adjust.* God never intended your life to be the same day in and day out. That would be boring! He sends challenges (someone or something that outweighs you!) so that you will mature in your faith—and so that your life will have some spice!

Two Steps Back

- Does your life today seem balanced or unbalanced?
- What do you think is weighing you down the most?

Two Steps Forward

- Read James 5:7–18.
- Write down things you may have to adjust in order to live a more balanced life.

One Step More

Dear God, help me to have peace and keep balanced by focusing on You. Teach me to trust and adjust. Amen.

Binding Your Sacrifice

*God... has given us light; Bind the sacrifice with
cords to the horns of the altar.*

Psalm 118:27 (NKJ)

Has God ever given you clear instructions, and then somewhere along the way you began to have second thoughts? Although you were certain of His leading at the time, doubts crept in. Perhaps what He asked you to do seemed impossible or illogical—in short, a sacrifice.

The psalmist tells us that once God has given us light on a certain matter, we are to bind any sacrifice involved on the "altar." In the early days of Hebrew worship, two altars were required. The golden altar was for incense offerings, and the brazen altar for burnt offerings. The latter was directly in front of the tabernacle's door. This symbolized the necessity for blood to be shed in order to enter the presence of a holy God.

The brazen altar was made with acacia wood overlaid with brass. It had rings and staves so it could be transported from place to place. On its upper corners were projections that resembled animal horns. Whenever a sacrifice was made, the blood of the animal was smeared on these, and sometimes the animal itself was tied to it with cords. Binding the carcass to the horns prevented any afterthoughts or stealing!

When someone acts on the light God has given them, no matter how difficult it may seem, they too are binding a sacrifice to the horns of their personal altar. They are relinquishing their right to change their mind.

You will never know the depths of God's love and faithfulness until you learn to trust Him even when it doesn't

167

make sense. Especially when it doesn't make sense. He delights in surprising His children, and His best is given to those who are willing to tie a few knots around their stubborn wills.

Two Steps Back

- Have you ever felt guided by God and then not followed through on your part?
- What happened when you did follow His guidance?

Two Steps Forward

- Read Proverbs 16:1–9.
- Do something today that indicates you are saying yes to God.

One Step More

Dear Father, forgive me if I have untied the ropes of Your will in my present circumstance. Help me to be willing to make whatever sacrifices are necessary for You to complete Your big plan in me. Please accept my offering to You today. Amen.

You are Loved

I have sought your face with all my heart;
be gracious to me according to your promise.

Psalm 119:58

At the age of seventeen, Ingvar Kamprad founded IKEA, the world's largest furniture store to date. Although he became a successful businessman and a billionaire, his accomplishments never altered who he was—"a big baggy man" bent on thriftiness, simplicity, and humility.

Ingvar knew the secret of keeping his employees and customers happy. He thought of his company as family and his customers as friends. He was generous with his hugs, and sought business improvements by conversing anonymously with his patrons.

Jesus, too, went unnoticed by many of the people He mingled with here on earth. Instead of insisting on respect, He listened to their needs. He asked simple questions. He read hearts. He loved. He hugged.

The thought of God coming to earth in human form is mind-boggling. He didn't need to land on our planet to know how we live. And He certainly didn't need our opinion about anything. So what was His motivation?

The Bible says, "For God so loved the world that he gave his one and only Son, that whoever believes in him shall not perish but have eternal life" (John 3:16). Simply put, He wants to have a love relationship with us so that we can spend eternity with Him. That's incredible!

Someone said, "Love is more easily demonstrated than defined." God didn't just tell us He loved us—He showed us. He did this by allowing his Son to die to meet the requirements for a relationship with a holy God. All we have to do is accept this provision and love Him back. This is the first step for true contentment with your life.

Two Steps Back

- Do you have a personal relationship with God through Jesus Christ?
- Have you confessed your sins to Him and asked for His forgiveness?

Two Steps Forward

- Read John 3:1–21.
- If you have never made the decision to accept Christ as your personal Savior, why not do so today?

One Step More

Dear Lord Jesus, thank You for loving me enough to die for me. Take my life and make it into something beautiful for You. Amen.

Attitude

For your name's sake, LORD, preserve my life;
in your righteousness, bring me out of trouble.

Psalm 143:11

Once I was on a committee to arrange hostesses for a large Christian conference. Our task was to assign volunteers to greet the attendees at the church entrances and to direct traffic to workshops.

The building had underground parking, and we needed someone stationed at an elevator in the garage to greet and direct the guests from that area. It wasn't the most desirable position. It would be far more pleasant to assign them all to the beautiful spacious church foyer where there was light and action! Finally, someone on the committee volunteered.

As I got out of my car in the garage for the conference's first session, I was impressed by the lone greeter. Well-dressed and all smiles, she warmly directed the women toward the elevator. It seemed like an insignificant job, but in reality she was many women's first impression of the conference. She was a happy face in a drab place.

Sometimes God will position you in a dark corner to brighten someone else's life. At the time all you may be able to see is your own misery. But it may not be about *you* at all. Oswald Chambers said, *"No healthy saint ever chooses suffering; he chooses God's will, as Jesus did, whether it means suffering or not... God plants His saints in the most useless places... where they will glorify Him, and we are not judges at all of where that is."*[42]

171

Your suffering at this moment may not make sense. One day you may know why this has happened. What's important today is your attitude. Instead of complaining, why not ask God to give you a thankful and trusting heart? Just switching the channel from "Poor me" to "Use me, God" will do you wonders.

Two Steps Back

- Can you think of a time in your life when God used you in a place you didn't want to be?
- Are you in that sort of place now?

Two Steps Forward

- Read Isaiah 55:6–13.
- Do something today for someone else. Record your actions—and the results—in your journal.

One Step More

Lord, You know I have lots of questions. Please help me to leave the answers in Your hands. Thank You that I am alive today, and that my reaction to my pain can be someone else's gain. Amen.

Picking Up the Pieces

You have been a shelter for me…

Psalm 61:3 (NKJ)

In the spring of 2017, a string of massive storms tore through several Southern states one weekend. Thousands of people hid in basements, closets, bathtubs, storm cellars, any place that could keep them safe. Clinging to one another, they listened in fear to the thunderous roar around them. What would happen to their homes and possessions? Would the lives of friends and relatives be spared?

When silence came, they emerged from their hiding places to face a world of devastation. Houses were leveled. Cars smashed. Debris was scattered everywhere.

The safe havens had spared the lives of most, but now they needed different shelters after the storm—physically, emotionally, and spiritually. Many had to start over from nothing. It would take time, money, patience—and a whole lot of courage.

You may have just survived a major storm in your life. Perhaps during your worst moments, the prayers and love of others sheltered you. However, you now have to pick up the pieces—and you will need some invaluable tools:

Prayer. Commit your situation to God. Place yourself under His protection. After presenting your petitions, listen to His instructions. Write down what He tells you.

Plan. No town is rebuilt in the aftermath of a tornado unless there is a plan. Prayerfully list your options. Talk to a positive spiritual leader. Confide in good friends. Then formulate a plan before you take action.

Patience. Someone once said, "Patience is the ability to throttle your motor when you feel like stripping the gears." The recovery process may take longer than you like. But remember Jesus is a finishing carpenter. He will spend what time it takes to make your life a piece of fine art—but He needs your cooperation.

Play. Take a break. Do something that will make you laugh. Watch a funny movie. Read a hilarious book. Go out with a friend who has a funny bone. Laughter will help you deal better with your fears and frustrations.

Proceed. You won't be able to reconstruct your life overnight. Don't try. Salvage the best to make something better—one piece at a time.

God didn't spare you to abandon you. Like the apostle Paul, you can say: "I can do everything through him who gives me the strength" (Philippians 4:13).

Two Steps Back

- How are you picking up the pieces of your life today?
- Do you depend more on your own strength and abilities or on God's?

Two Steps Forward

- Read Luke 12:22–34.
- List the headings *Patience, Plan, Prayer, Play,* and *Proceed* in your journal. After each entry write down ideas concerning a particular problem you are facing.

One Step More

God, please help me have patience as I carry out Your recovery plan for me. Help me to proceed prayerfully. Amen.

Crumbs

Those who know your name trust in you,
for you, LORD, have never forsaken those who seek you.

Psalm 9:10

This morning while gazing out our kitchen window, I noticed two ducks, a male and a female, were waddling across the backyard in search of food. I quickly reached for a crust of bread and headed for the deck.

I only had to toss one small morsel, and in seconds the mallards were below me on the grass. As I dropped the pieces, they quickly snatched them up, bumping into each other in the process.

A couple hours later, I took a break from writing and returned to the kitchen window. The ducks had long disappeared, but a few starlings were pecking at the grass in the same vicinity. They seemed to be feasting on the crumbs left behind.

This reminded me of a strange little story in the Bible. Jesus and his disciples were on a road trip through Tyre. Jesus wanted to keep their arrival a secret, but word soon spread that the famous teacher from Nazareth was in town. They had no sooner arrived then a woman fell at Jesus's feet, begging for Him to heal her daughter who was demon-possessed.

At first, Jesus seemed to ignore her. This annoyed His disciples because she wouldn't let up, and they wanted Him to at least send her away. "I was only sent to the lost sheep of Israel," he told them. "It is not right to take the children's bread and toss it to their dogs."

"Yes, Lord," she said, "but even the dogs eat the crumbs that fall under their masters' table."

"You have great faith!" Jesus answered her. "Your request is granted" (Matt. 15:22–28).

The lesson here is that Jesus, the Bread of Life, came to nourish both Jews and Gentiles. He is the same source of substance for everyone. And that should encourage you. Don't get discouraged if He seems to be working miracles in the lives of others—and not in yours. They may seem to be feasting, but don't forget the crumbs! God will allow just the right amount to fall to meet your needs.

Two Steps Back

- Do you think God has favorites?
- Do you ever feel you are not as worthy as someone else to receive a blessing from God?

Two Steps Forward

- Read Philippians 4:1–7.
- Is there something you have neglected to pray for because you felt unworthy? If so, write your request to God—and be specific!

One Step More

Dear Lord, help me to remember that You don't have favorites—and that You are the Bread of my life. Even a crumb of You is enough. Amen.

Best Guide

Your word is a lamp for my feet,
a light on my path.

Psalm 119:105

Years ago I was facing a life-changing decision. There were definite pros and cons to the situation, and I had no idea which way to turn.

Conflicting emotions struggled within me as I fingered the pages of my well-worn Bible. Over the years this one book has given me sound guidance. Now I scanned its underlined words like a cook seeking a no-fail recipe.

Our verse today caught my attention. "That's all fine and good," I muttered to myself, "but I don't have the time or energy right now to search the scriptures. There must be an easier way than this."

I put down my Bible and picked up the phone. If anyone could give me spiritual advice, it would be Edna. She was older and closer to God than most people I knew. Perhaps He would give her a word for me.

When I told Edna my story, there was a short silence on the other end of the line. "Cathy," she finally said. "I feel that the Lord's *Word* is a lamp for your feet, and a light for your path."

Had I heard right? Edna quoted the only Bible passage I had read that morning! A tingling sensation went through my body as I thanked her and hung up the phone.

I have never forgotten the lesson I learned that day—God sometimes uses people and circumstances to guide us, but His most frequent method is through His Word. How much easier it would be if He would speak to us audibly—or if we could just pick up the phone or e-mail Him! But God is not into laziness or shortcuts.

I took up my Bible again. I was now prepared to spend time to hear God's voice through His written Word. Eventually I read a portion that gave me specific direction. The "light to my path" brought me the peace I so desperately needed.[43]

Two Steps Back

- Do you set aside time each day to read a portion of the Bible?
- Are there certain verses or passages that have given you specific guidance?

Two Steps Forward

- Read Psalm 119:9–16.
- Start a scripture and prayer journal if you haven't already. Write down the verses you read and comment on them. Also record your prayer requests—and how they were answered!

One Step More

Dear God, thank You for giving us the Bible. Help me to read it and apply it to my life. And may Your Spirit guide me to the path You want me to follow. Amen.

One of a Kind

For you created my inmost being;
you knit me together in my mother's womb.

Psalm 139:13

I first heard about Millie Stamm when I became involved in Stonecroft Ministries, an interdenominational evangelism ministry, a number of years ago. For forty years, Millie was in charge of the organization's prayer ministry and was highly respected by all those who knew her.

Millie was a tiny lady with a giant faith. Although she never thought of herself as a writer, she wrote devotional material that inspired millions of people around the world. She was the sort of person that people came to for prayer because she seemed to have a special contact with God. She loved others, and they loved her.

All those involved in the ministry were deeply saddened by Millie's death in 1999. At her memorial service, Meryl Bishop, the woman who was assigned to take her place as the prayer leader, commented, "I can never be Millie Stamm. But I can be available, like Millie was. I can be yielded, like Millie was. And I can be obedient to God, like Millie was."

So often in life we feel like failures because we don't seem to measure up to someone we admire or to standards set by a certain group of people. I met Meryl a few years ago, and she had no resemblance to Millie. She did have, however, the same zeal for Christ, the same desire to be whatever He wanted her to be.

Don't compare yourself to someone else. When God knit you in your mother's womb, He didn't use a pattern. His design for your life is yours alone. You can be inspired and motivated by other people, but you will never be them. You will even receive one-of-a-kind trials! That's because He isn't finished "knitting" you yet; His needles are still clicking!

Two Steps Back

- Do you ever get discouraged by comparing yourself to someone else?
- Do you look at others and envy them because their circumstances seem much better than yours?

Two Steps Forward

- Read Isaiah 46.
- Ask a close friend what they feel is unique about you, and then make your own list of positive traits.

One Step More

Lord, forgive me if I've thought less of myself by comparing myself to _____. Help me to remember that You have a beautiful plan for my life—and that You are still working on it. Amen.

Giants

Notice good people, observe the righteous...

Psalm 37:37 (Good News)

We can learn much from noticing and observing good-living people. This doesn't mean we put them on a pedestal where they can do no wrong. Nor should we copy their every move and agree with everything they say. But a good Christian is worth watching!

My mother was the first major spiritual influence in my life. She not only taught her three daughters Christian disciplines, she practiced them. We tiptoed around her every morning as she silently read her well-worn Bible and prayed in her rocking chair. She never missed church. "Working for the Lord" was her life ambition. All of these customs rubbed off on me.

I have admired and observed many other outstanding Christians in my lifetime. One that probably influenced me more than most was Jess Horlacher, a childhood neighbor.

Jess took a keen interest in her neighbors—especially their kids. She arranged hayrides, ice-skating and sledding parties, chili feeds, Christmas caroling, you name it. Her door always was open. She believed in the power of warm cookies, peanut brittle, and hugs.

The woman on the farm over the hill taught me to imitate Jesus Christ. I could never put down another person around Jess. She wouldn't stand for it. Gossiping, and any other form of negative thinking, stopped outside her door. "Love one another" was her motto. This was especially true in her home—which was not always easy. I watched closely—and learned.

As you think about those Christians who have influenced you the most, think how they might handle the trial you are presently experiencing. And then ask yourself, "What would Jesus do?"

Two Steps Back

- Do you know any Christian giants? What have you admired about them? Why?
- Do you know their "secret" for spiritual success?

Two Steps Forward

- Read Ruth 1.
- Contact one Christian you admire. Thank them for their influence on your life, and then ask them what, or who, has made them who they are.

One Step More

Lord, thank You for the good people You have placed in my life. Help me to learn from them. And may I live in such a way that others will want to follow in my footsteps as well. Amen.

Path to Freedom

*Have mercy on me, O God,
according to your unfailing love;
according to your great compassion
blot out my transgressions.*

Psalm 51:1

Heartaches seem to double when you are partially to blame—and admitting one's part never comes easy. Even if all your relatives and friends have sided with you, you still have to live with your conscience. Truth will never hide under the rock of pride for very long. Once exposed, the fastest way to heal is through forgiveness.

First, you need to be forgiven by God. In the Bible, forgiveness and confession go hand in hand. Although Christ has already paid the price for your sins, you are required to present, or confess, your wrongdoings to Him in exchange for forgiveness. The psalmist said, "When I kept quiet, my bones wasted away" (Psalm 32:3). Sin that is not dealt with will eventually take a toll on both body and soul.

Secondly, you need to come clean with whomever you have hurt. Even if that person will not forgive you, you have done your part. Sometimes one act of contrition can bring peace to all parties involved.

Then look in the mirror and say, "I forgive you."

I was never so self-absorbed as I was during the first year of separation from my first husband. The rejection by someone I loved and trusted was devastating. The fact that I had contributed to the failure of our marriage was even more painful.

I couldn't face that for several years because it hurt so much. Healing came only after I forgave my ex-husband—and especially myself.

You, too, can find relief from your grief through forgiveness—with God's help. Ponder His words to the prophet Jeremiah: "Is there anything too hard for me" (Jer. 32:27)?

Two Steps Back

- Can you think of anything you have done that has contributed to your present heartache?
- Is this possibility difficult for you to admit?

Two Steps Forward

- Read Psalm 51.
- Write in your journal how you may have added fuel to the fire of a bad situation in which you are presently involved.

One Step More

Dear Father, You alone know all my pain today. You also know how difficult it is for me to admit that some of this may be my fault. Please give me courage to deal with the truth one step at a time. You have promised that truth will set me free—and I need to be free. Amen.

Secrets

But who can discern their own errors?
Forgive my hidden faults.

Psalm 19:12

The best-known species of the myrtle plant is a moderate-sized tree with small white or pink flowers. Its thick, shiny leaves possess tiny glands that produce a lovely fragrance. The leaves of this not-so-spectacular plant need to be crushed, however, in order to get a good whiff of the aromatic perfume.

We often don't know what we are made of until faced with a crisis—until we are crushed, so to speak. We may be somewhat aware of certain weaknesses, and have been hiding our "true self" for years. Unfortunately, these "hidden faults" quite often surface under pressure. The apostle Peter called it "the hidden person of the heart" (1 Peter 3:4, NKJ).

On the other hand, we may discover strengths we had no idea we possessed. Like the myrtle leaves, we may find that we actually smell better under pressure! In other words, our heartaches in life can bring out the worst or the best in all of us.

The good news is that any revelation of a "hidden fault" can serve as an opportunity to face a particular weakness head-on. Admitting you are not perfect is the first step toward recovery.

Once you face the truth about yourself, pray as the psalmist did to be cleansed from your secret sins (maybe now not so hidden!). This means asking for forgiveness and then turning—with God's help—in a new direction.

I have discovered over the years that if I don't deal with a certain weakness within myself when it is first presented, I usually face it again somewhere down the line. If it has been dealt with properly the first time around, it makes the next crisis much easier. Like the myrtle leaves, I come out smelling pretty good!

Two Steps Back

- Have you made some discoveries about yourself in the past few days and months?
- If so, did those discoveries make you feel proud or discouraged?

Two Steps Forward

- Read Psalm 19.
- Write in your journal any discoveries you have made recently about yourself.

One Step More

God, help me to remember that You would never allow me to be crushed unless there was a good reason. Help me to face this challenge with courage—and to forgive myself if I have not been perfect. Amen.

Dealing with Guilt

Then I acknowledged my sin to you
and did not cover up my iniquity.
I said, "I will confess
my transgressions to the LORD."
And you forgave
the guilt of my sin.

Psalm 32:5

Once you confess your sins to God, you may need to deal with guilt. Like burning embers after a forest fire, guilt needs to be snuffed out (stamped on!) so no further damage is done.

Guilt does not benefit anyone. Clinging to regret and remorse delays recovery more than anything else. It gives the sense of unfinished business—over which you have no control. The "if only" syndrome will only fan the flames. It will rob you of peace and keep you from getting on with your life.

In his book, *The Gift of Hope: How We Survive Our Tragedies*, Dr. Robert Veninga states, *"Sometimes other people need to give us permission to rid ourselves of guilt. But most of the time we need to forgive ourselves. How do you diminish guilt? Unfortunately, there is no easy formula, no sure guarantee. Guilt is one of the strongest and most difficult emotions to conquer."*[44]

I believe a follower of Jesus Christ has an edge here. The Bible says, "If we confess our sins to him, he can be depended on to forgive us and to cleanse us from every wrong" (1 John 1:9, TLB). If we truly believe that He has wiped the slate clean, we don't have a good enough reason to hang on to guilt.

To diminish guilt, remind yourself that if God has forgiven you, you must forgive yourself. God's forgiveness is only possible because Jesus Christ paid for the penalty of your sins. His shed blood is enough. You cannot use guilt as a penance. The price has been paid. Period.

Then remind yourself that you are human. You are not perfect, and you never will be. Remember life does go on. As Alexander Graham Bell once noted, *"When one door closes, another opens, but we often look so long and regretfully upon the closed door that we do not see the one that has opened for us."*[45]

Two Steps Back

- Think about all your good qualities that others admire.
- You may have made mistakes recently, but what have you done *right*?

Two Steps Forward

- Read Psalm 32.
- Make a list of what you feel you have done right in your current situation.

One Step More

Dear Lord, help me to deal with these feelings of guilt. Since You have forgiven me, may I forgive myself. And show me what door You are opening for me now. Amen.

For His Sake

For the sake of your name, LORD,
forgive my iniquity, though it is great.

Psalm 25:11

I will never forget the time I prayed this prayer—and really meant it. As the result of some deep emotional and spiritual needs, I was not living a godly lifestyle at the time.

One afternoon I drove to a secluded area, parked my car, and faced myself head on. I thought about how my actions could have a detrimental effect on those who knew I claimed to be a Christian. For the first time, I acknowledged that I was in a position to hurt Jesus and what He was trying to accomplish in the lives of those in my world.

I leaned over the steering wheel of my car and sobbed. I begged God to forgive me and not to allow my actions to cause harm to His cause. "For *Your* sake, please help me!" I wailed.

The psalmist David must have felt the same way. He honestly didn't want God to get a bad rap for what he had done. He knew that the sooner he came clean with Him, the sooner God could accomplish His purposes.

There is always a ripple effect. Throw love and forgiveness into the waters of your world, and others will be blessed and helped. Toss in disobedience, selfishness—any sin—and those around you will suffer. And that suffering ultimately hurts the cause of Jesus Christ.

If Jesus means anything to you, if you claim Him as your Lord and Savior, then the relationship you have with Him should stir you to action. It is of utmost importance for you to deal with the issue of forgiveness—not just for *your* sake, but for *His* sake.

First of all, seek His forgiveness for any wrong you've committed. Then forgive those who have wronged you. And then forgive yourself. When these three areas are cleared, God can then work His purposes in your life once more.

I have thanked God over and over for forgiving me—and for giving me another chance to be His vessel. He has had to repair some big cracks, but He is using me once again. To Him I give all the praise!

Two Steps Back

- How much do you think your life influences those around you?
- Do you think your current circumstances can influence others to believe—or not believe—in Jesus Christ?

Two Steps Forward

- Read Psalm 25.
- Make a list of those closest to you. Think about how your actions may be affecting each one on a spiritual level.

One Step More

Dear Lord, I don't want to continue to hurt You and those I love by my actions. Please forgive me, and help me to forgive _____—and myself. Amen.

Why Forgive?

Restore to me the joy of your salvation
and grant me a willing spirit, to sustain me.

Psalm 51:12

Forgiving someone who has hurt you is not easy. I know. It took me several years to forgive a friend who betrayed me. I dealt with it in various ways: no contact with her, not mentioning her name, not thinking about the incident, keeping myself busy, pretending I had forgiven her. But the "joy of my salvation" was not restored until God gave me a "willing spirit" to forgive.

You may be thinking (as I did!):

1. I'd be admitting they are right—and they aren't!
2. I would be condoning what they have done.
3. I shouldn't have to forgive them if they haven't asked for forgiveness.
4. I don't want to forget what they've done—ever!
5. Justice must be served.
6. If I forgive them, they may repeat it.

Why then should you forgive? First, because *you* have been forgiven. Christ paid a huge price for *your* pardon. Oswald Chambers put it this way: *"Forgiveness is the divine miracle of grace; it cost God the Cross of Jesus Christ before He could forgive sin and remain a holy God."*[46]

Once you accept God's grace, He requires you to extend that same mercy to others. "If you do not forgive men (or women) their sins, your Father will not forgive your sins" (Matt. 6:14). Strong words!

Clinging to certain memories like a dirty shredded security blanket doesn't produce Christian maturity. The abundant life Christ promised will never truly be yours until you forgive—and let go.

I prayed for help (more like HELP!) to forgive my friend. One day I encountered her, and I knew I was free. It was like the incident had never happened. The moment I hugged her, we both knew "the divine miracle of grace" had taken place.

You, too, can know God's strength and power to forgive. Just ask!

Two Steps Back

- Is there someone in your life whom you've never been able to forgive?
- If so, why do you find the idea of forgiving her (or him) difficult?

Two Steps Forward

- Read Matthew 6:9–15.
- Start a "Journey to Forgiveness" section in your journal. Write down your reasons for not forgiving a certain person. And then write out a prayer asking God to help you with this specific situation.

One Step More

Lord, You know how very difficult it is for me to forgive _____. Please give me Your grace to do what I cannot do on my own. Amen.

Forgiving the Minors

*The righteous person may have many troubles,
but the LORD delivers him from them all.*

Psalm 34:19

There are major and minor players in a tragedy. The major players are easy to spot: the husband who left his wife for another woman, the drunk driver who killed a couple on their way to church, the mother who gambled her family into poverty, the doctor who prescribed the wrong medication.

The minor players are the people who insist on giving unwanted advice, the inconsiderate funeral director, the unethical insurance woman, the friends who suddenly disappear, the relatives who just don't understand, the creditors who won't go away.

Forgiving the minor players is part of the healing process. Even though they had nothing to do with the crisis itself, they have added to your misery. It's unfortunate, but they too must be added to your "those-I-should-forgive" list.

When I was undergoing cancer treatments, I was challenged to deal with a few minor players. There was the friend who never called or sent me a get-well wish. The young night nurse who gave me too many pills and too many frowns. The doctor who did an unnecessary painful procedure. The relative who disagreed with my treatment.

For some reason, the minor players have been allowed on the team. We don't want them, but nevertheless they are there. I had to learn to downplay the actions of the inconsiderate and the unkind. Even to forgive. Once you stare death in the face, you realize that life is too short to sweat the small stuff.

Have you found yourself stressed out by the minor players? Why not tell God all about it? Why not ask for His guidance and peace. Why not forgive?

Two Steps Back

- Have you been hurt by the actions of others?
- Would you consider these major or minor players?

Two Steps Forward

- Read Psalm 34.
- Zero in on one of these "minor players." Make a covenant with yourself and God to forgive this person.

One Step More

Dear Lord, You know how _____ has bothered me. Please show me how to handle this situation— and how to forgive. I long for Your peace and patience. Amen.

A Better View

*Open my eyes that I may see
wonderful things in your law.*

Psalm 119:18

Several years ago we decided to cut down a tree in our front yard. It wasn't an easy decision. The large pine had dominated our small yard for many years.

The tree was taller than our two-story house. Its presence gave me the feeling of privacy and protection. To Allen, it meant work.

Every time he mowed the lawn, he had to pick up pinecones first. Raking needles and trimming branches was a nuisance. Now the tree's large roots were cracking our driveway's pavement.

I was away the day the tree came down. That evening as I drove into our yard, the empty space in front of the house seemed almost eerie. The "bareness" made me feel like the whole world was looking at us.

But I was in for a treat. Our view from the living room window was drastically changed. We now could see the mountains and the twinkling lights of a ski hill. Far away skyscrapers shimmered in the morning sunshine and glowed at night. We could see, not just hear, children playing in the park and neighbors walking their dogs.

Our verse today asks God to open our eyes to all the wonderful things He has in store for us. Unfortunately, sometimes He can't answer that prayer because something or someone is blocking our view.

Unforgiveness is perhaps one of the largest obstacles that block one's view of God's blessings. But He will not force us to forgive. We have to make that choice and then act on it in order for us to once more see life from His perspective. The view can be fantastic!

Two Steps Back

- Is there an obstacle in your life that is obstructing your vision of God and what He wants to do for you?
- Are you picking up pinecones when you could be basking in the beauty of His power and love?

Two Steps Forward

- Read Psalm 119:1–16.
- Make a list of those things that may be obstructing your "view."

One Step More

Lord, help me to recognize any obstacles in my life that may be obstructing my view of Your best for me. Help me deal with any bad attitudes or habits that block me from seeing my potential and Your power. And help me to forgive. Amen.

Nothing to Prove

Let my vindication come from you;
may your eyes see what is right.

Psalm 17:2

When Caren's husband left her for another woman, she was deeply wounded. Rejected and abandoned by the man she loved and trusted for almost twenty years, she didn't think she could handle the pain. Thoughts of revenge often popped up out of nowhere. She knew she could make his life miserable.

Fortunately, she did not give in to the temptation to retaliate. Deep down she knew it would do more damage than good. She also knew it was not God's way of doing things.

First of all, God "sees what is right." We don't have to prove anything. He knows every tiny detail of what's happened to us. He knows who is right, who is wrong—and why.

Secondly, He tells us in scripture to leave all revenge in His capable hands (Deut. 32:35; Psalms 94:1; Romans 12:19; Hebrews 10:30). If vindication is in order, He will see that it is done.

If unattended, emotional wounds can turn into bitterness. Someone said, "The root of bitterness is hate; the symptom of bitterness is sarcasm; the result of bitterness is manipulation." Revenge is manipulation. Nowhere does God give us permission to orchestrate another person's life. We are only told to love—and forgive.

Dr. James Dobson wrote, "*Psychologists and ministers now agree that there is only one cure for bitterness. It is to forgive.... Only when we find the emotional maturity to release those who*

198

have wronged us, whether they have repented or not, will the wounds finally start to heal."[47]

Jesus said, "And when you stand praying, if you hold anything against anyone, forgive him, so that your Father in heaven may forgive you your sins" (Mark 11:25). He leaves no other options. Forgiveness paves the way for healing.

Two Steps Back

- Have you ever felt like getting even with someone big time?
- If you followed through, what were the results?

Two Steps Forward

- Read Romans 12:17–21.
- Make plans to do a good deed for the person who has hurt you.

One Step More

Lord, I have no idea how I am going to forgive _____.
I know I can't do it on my own. Please help me to be willing to allow You to work this out within me. I need all the help You can give me. Amen.

A Good Habit

O God, You are my God;
Early will I seek You.

Psalm 63:1 (NKJ)

Oswald Chambers said, *"Get into the habit of dealing with God about everything. Unless in the first waking moment of the day you learn to fling the door wide back and let God in, you will work on a wrong level all day; but swing the door wide open and pray to your Father in secret, and every public thing will be stamped with the presence of God."*[48]

I've spent most of my life fighting with that door! Although I was raised in a Christian family where personal devotions were greatly encouraged, I've always struggled with this spiritual discipline (and it *is* a discipline!).

As a teenager, reading my Bible before school seemed impossible, so sometimes I tried it *at* school—which got me into trouble. As a young adult, my husband and children needed my attention. I would sometimes try to have an alone time with God behind a bedroom or bathroom door (preferably a locked one!). The kids left home, and I went to work. Squeezing prayer time in became even more of a challenge.

Finally I discovered—while working outside the home—that the secret was to rise early! I set the alarm for 6:30, which gave me time to read my Bible and a devotional—and pray. I also used the half-hour drive to work for more prayer.

This routine did exactly what Oswald Chambers said it would do. My days became "stamped with the presence of God." I was going through some difficulties during that time, and I quickly realized I needed God with me at all times—and our early-morning rendezvous was the key.

Do you meet with God through prayer and Bible reading on a regular basis? It doesn't have to be early mornings, of course. But it will help if you start each day by at least opening your door to His love and presence.

Two Steps Back

- What is your greatest challenge in finding time for consistent scripture reading and prayer?
- How determined are you to make this a priority in your life?

Two Steps Forward

- Read Psalm 119:57–64.
- To help yourself to improve in this area, mark on a calendar the times you spend with God in prayer and meditation.

One Step More

Dear Lord, thank You for providing me with ways to overcome the obstacles in my life. Help me to meet with You on a regular basis for my nourishment—and marching orders. Amen.

Gratitude Attitude

It is good to praise the LORD
and make music to your name, O Most High.
Psalm 92:1

After ten years of living with continual pain as the result of a climbing mishap in the Sierras, Tim Hansel wrote a book entitled *You Gotta Keep Dancin'*. In it he wrote: *"Perhaps the most important thing that I have learned in my journey with pain is the intrinsic value of life itself—the sacredness of each unrepeatable moment. To partake of it is sheer gift; none of us did anything to deserve it. The most tangible form of grace itself is the substance of our normal everyday life."*[49]

Tim had learned one of the greatest secrets to enduring heartaches—thankfulness. When you can find good—any good—in your trials, you are turning a negative into a positive. Negative thinking is lethal in a crisis. It will sap you of the physical, mental, and spiritual energy you need to cope.

Thankfulness, on the other hand, is positive. Since positive and negative thoughts cannot coexist, thankfulness energizes your mind for productivity. It enables you to consider other possibilities besides your problems. It produces faith.

A grateful heart benefits you more than God. The Almighty isn't some neurotic superpower who needs acknowledgement from His creations in order to feel validated. His character is love. And in His love for you, He knows what is best for you. He also desires to have a love relationship with you. Just as an ungrateful child cannot enjoy a happy healthy relationship with a parent, you cannot experience kinship to your heavenly Father if you have not developed a "gratitude attitude."

Gratitude is the cart that will carry your faith. By acknowledging the goodness of God, you are positioning yourself for Him to work in your life and in your circumstances. Don't dwell on your losses. Be thankful for all the positive things in your life. It *is* good for you!

Two Steps Back

- Do you think you have a "gratitude attitude?"
- Are you in the habit of thanking God after the end of each day for the good things He has brought your way?

Two Steps Forward

- Read Psalm 135.
- Look for the not-so-obvious things for which to be thankful. List them in your journal.

One Step More

Dear God, help me to turn my negatives into positives this day. Thank You for all the wonderful possibilities it holds for me. Give me a grateful heart and giving hands. Amen.

Motivation

But as for me, I am poor and needy;
may the Lord think of me.
You are my help and my deliverer;
you are my God, do not delay.

Psalm 40:17

I was in the middle of applying my makeup one morning when the phone rang. Friends, two couples that I had not seen in years, were in our city for a few hours and wanted to stop by. I was delighted—and knew my work was cut out for me. I figured I had about forty minutes to get the house and myself ready.

Allen says I have two speeds—slow and fast. I'm prone to be slow, but am quite capable of speed when motivated. That morning I almost stripped my gears as I shifted into high. Nothing motivates me to houseclean faster than company coming—especially out-of-town company!

I'm sure the good Lord was laughing. I was like a mad woman as I whipped around my place! I swooped up the bills and paperwork off the kitchen table, cleaned out the dishwasher, loaded the dishwasher, wiped down counters, swept floors, scrubbed a toilet, stashed away TV trays, washed spots off windows, dusted furniture, changed my clothes, applied makeup, brewed a pot of coffee, arranged a plate of cookies—and even had time to spare!

I am often reminded how well God knows me. I am not a self-starter, so He sometimes motivates me to do His will in some pretty creative ways! Some of the things He has allowed to come my way have not been pleasant (I *do* like visitors!), but I know He always has my best interest in mind. I just need a little shove from time to time.

God knows what will motivate *you* to fulfill His purposes in *your* life. His nudges come in various forms, and you may not always appreciate them. When trouble knocks on your door, you may need to clean up your act—fast. Instead of complaining and refusing to cooperate, you will benefit the most by thanking Him for the motivation.

Two Steps Back

- What motivates you the most into action?
- Can you see some of your problems as perhaps nudges from God to either help you draw closer to Him or to go in a new direction?

Two Steps Forward

- Read Psalm 73:21–28.
- Write in your journal the ways you feel God has been guiding you.

One Step More

Dear Lord, I may not always like the way You motivate me to action, so help me to cooperate—without questioning. Amen.

Daily Blessings

The LORD will watch over your coming and going
both now and forevermore.

Psalm 121:8

Life goes on in spite of our heartaches. Bills must be paid, lawns mowed, groceries bought, laundry done, flowers watered. What may seem a bother right now may actually be a blessing in disguise. An everyday chore or routine:

Distracts you from your pain. My friend Louise e-mailed me shortly after a chemotherapy treatment. She said a severe allergic reaction almost caused her death that day. But she concluded, "Anyway, I came home, ate supper, ate some raspberries from the bushes and feel just fine!!! So there!!"

Even though your problems won't go away, having to cope with the necessities in life will momentarily get your mind working in another direction. Any small patch of peace will help toward healing.

Gives you structure. When things seem out of whack, be thankful for the mundane that gives your life some semblance of structure. Performing even a small routine task will help you feel more in control. At a time when you may feel helpless and useless, doing a necessary chore can keep you sane.

Keeps you functioning. Years ago, when I was in the throes of depression, I found it very difficult to do even the simplest of tasks. I wandered through my days in a fog. I had little energy or drive, and I cried at the drop of a hat. And then I remembered it was spring, and I should be planting flowers by the house. Slowly and methodically I got out the garden tools and set to work. Digging in the soil and planting a few petunias did something to my psyche. I was doing something useful; I was creating beauty in my world. It also reminded me that spring follows every winter.

Reminds you that life goes on. Motivations like eating, bathing, and taking the dog for a walk can get you to keep going in spite of how you may feel. Thank God you have these activities right now. They are a constant reminder that the wheels of everyday life keep turning in spite of your pain. Tomorrow the sun will shine again—and so will you.

Two Steps Back

- How have your recent problems affected your daily routine?
- Have you been neglecting basic things like eating well, bathing, housecleaning, or taking care of your children?

Two Steps Forward

- Read Psalm 121.
- Make a "To Do" list. You will feel better when you begin ticking off your accomplishments!

One Step More

Dear God, forgive me if I have complained about all my unfinished tasks. Help me to see them as Your way of helping me through my pain. Give me strength to do what is before me today. Amen.

Confirmation

Give me a sign of your goodness,
that my enemies may see it and be put to shame,
for you, LORD, have helped me and comforted me.

Psalm 86:17

When I was twenty-five, our family was living in a remote town in northern British Columbia, Canada. The children were babies and times were tough. I became very lonely and discouraged.

I awoke late one night to feelings of frustration and self-pity. A verse from the Bible suddenly flashed across my mind. I had not been thinking about God, but there it was. I was only vaguely familiar with the scripture, and I couldn't recall ever memorizing it. In fact, I had no idea where it was in the Bible. And yet, at that moment I *knew* every word: *"Call unto me, and I will answer thee, and show thee great and mighty things, which thou knowest not."*[50]

Was God trying to get my attention? Was He telling me that good things were going to happen if I turned my problems over to Him? I had to find out!

I jumped out of bed and found my Bible. "If I just heard from You, God," I whispered, "please let me find that verse!"

I didn't have a clue where to look, so I just opened my Bible at random. A chill ran through my body when I found myself staring at the very words I'd just "seen."

I did call on God that night for a particular concern. My prayers weren't answered immediately, but eventually I did experience "great and mighty things!"

I've come to believe that confirmations—or signs—are sometimes His way of making sure we get His message. Amy Carmichael, the well-known missionary to India, wrote:

"When a word from the Lord comes to us twice about the same time, it is for some special purpose. It helps and challenges us. What makes the help so vital is the belief that it did not just 'happen,' but was planned by our tender Lord, who knows all about us. It is very wonderful, and very comforting, to know that He who has so much to think of is actually thinking about me."[51]

Don't be afraid to ask the Lord for a confirmation if you think He is taking you in a certain direction. He wants you to know His will. It is in His best interest—and yours—for you to follow Him with confidence.

Two Steps Back

- Can you think of a time when you felt God was guiding you because of a reoccurring incident?
- Have you asked God to give you confirmation if you are seeking His guidance at this time?

Two Steps Forward

- Read John 16:5–15.
- Write down your prayer for guidance in a particular matter and record any "answers" you may receive. Take note of any duplicates!

One Step More

Dear God, thank You for being concerned about every detail of my life. Help me to listen for Your instructions—and look for confirmations when I am in doubt. Amen.

Alone

He will deliver...him who has no helper.

Psalm 72:12 (NKJ)

Enduring heartbreak is a solitary experience. Even if you have support from family and friends, you basically have to come to terms with it on your own. Dr. Seuss puts it well in his children's book, *Oh, the Places You'll Go*:
All Alone!
Whether you like it or not,
Alone will be something
You'll be quite a lot.
And when you're alone, there's a very good chance,
You'll meet things that scare you
right out of your pants,
There are some, down the road between hither
and yon,
that can scare you so much you won't
want to go on.
But on you will go...[52]

It is quite common for a sudden loss or change in life to trigger a feeling of aloneness. This is part of being human, and no one is immune. Loneliness has been described as "a sense of emptiness, of feeling disconnected or alone, even in a crowd. Often it's accompanied by sadness, resentment and anxiety."

Our scripture today promises deliverance from God to "him who has no helper," the one who is feeling lonely. Is that you?

If so, remember His assistance comes in a variety of forms—and in ways that may surprise you. How you respond is up to you.

You can choose to crawl further into your shell of despair, or you can opt for His companionship and suggestions to dispel the negatives. In His plan, your crisis may be the very thing that will open up fresh opportunities for you, new doors to a more fulfilling life. You may feel alone in your particular situation, but with Him beside you, *on you will go...*

Two Steps Back

- Has there been a time in your life when you felt lonely?
- Do you feel alone today?

Two Steps Forward

- Read Psalm 62.
- Ask God to give you one friend who will help you in this particular situation—and then keep your eyes open!

One Step More

Dear God, You know how lonely I sometimes feel. Please give me a sense of Your presence today. Help me to remember that You have promised never to leave me. Amen.

Aspirin or Applesauce

I will behave wisely...

Psalm 101:2 (NKJ)

I left a message on my sister's answering machine one day asking for a recipe for applesauce. When she later returned my call, I proceeded to talk to her about my aches and pains.

"I thought you wanted to talk to me about applesauce," she said jokingly. "Maybe you should write a book entitled *Applesauce and the Other Important Things in Life*."

I agreed with her that that would be a great title, and that I had strayed from the main purpose of my call to her.

Allen had hinted for some time that I needed to do something with the apples from our tree that were going soft. I had made applesauce before but remembered having problems getting it to the right consistency. My sister Carolyn, the fruit and veggie expert, was the person I thought would know. It just so happened applesauce and aspirin were on the agenda for the same day.

I went to see my doctor that afternoon. As it turned out, my pains were not all that big of a deal. I should have concentrated more on the applesauce. Looking back, I'm sure cooking the fruit sauce would have been a good distraction—especially when I knew how pleased my husband would be!

Is this an aspirin day for you? Why not ask God to help you make applesauce? Find something creative and fun to do. Better yet, work on a project that will benefit someone else. It's amazing how life gets better when we get our minds off our troubles and onto something productive.

Two Steps Back

- What can you do today that will distract you from your problems?
- Can you think of an activity that you enjoy but have neglected lately?

Two Steps Forward

- Read Psalm 107:1–9.
- Do something today for someone else. Make a phone call, send a card, or pay someone a visit.

One Step More

Lord, help me to think about something else besides my problems today. Please give me ideas that will fill this day with pleasure and purpose. Amen.

Natural Highs

I rejoice in your promise
like one who finds great spoil.
Psalm 119:162

In the psalmist's day, rejoicing over great spoil would refer to a soldier's excitement when he was able to collect a valuable sword, shield, or whatever from a fallen enemy. A rather morbid form of treasure hunting, but a reality nevertheless. The larger the "spoil," the greater the thrill—or high.

The other day I received an e-mail with the heading "Natural Highs." It listed forty-one ways to have a euphoric experience, with "falling in love" as number one. Others were:

Laughing so hard your face hurts.
Finding a $20 bill in your coat from last winter.
Swinging on swings.
Spending time with close friends.
Watching the sunrise.

I thought about my own "natural highs." Discovering a certain first-edition book in an antique store. A publisher's acceptance letter. Chatting with an old friend. A spring bouquet from Allen or one of my children.

Answered prayers, however, are at the top of the list. I can't think of a better "high" than watching God transform someone for whom I have been praying. Whenever I realize He is working in a difficult situation, I'm in for some excitement!

When you are low, the tendency may be to turn to medication or physical activities for an upper. These may be good, but don't neglect the treasure at your fingertips. Discovering the reality of

God through His Word is one of the best "natural highs" you can receive.

Like a soldier enjoying the spoils of war, we need to have some moments of merriment in the middle of our battles. We need a "high" now and then. We can experience these if we are open to the surprises God brings our way. Watching the sun rise—or set—counts.

Two Steps Back

- What do you like to do for pleasure?
- What gives you your biggest "natural high?"

Two Steps Forward

- Read Psalm 119:161–168.
- Make a list of the things that make you feel happy inside.

One Step More

Dear God, thank You for the excitement You bring to my life in various forms. Help me to look for the "highs" You bring my way. And help me to remember that Your Word is full of treasures just waiting for me to find. Amen.

A Gift

You have kept me alive...

Psalm 30:3 (NKJ)

Delia felt totally helpless and useless as she sat beside her older brother's bedside.

How long had Bill been in intensive care now? Fourteen, fifteen weeks? Day after day she watched her sibling fight death. She told him repeatedly that she cared and loved him and that someday he'd be better. Was she offering him false hope?

As a Christian, Delia didn't believe in assisted suicide or euthanasia. The thought of taking someone's life for any reason just hadn't existed—until now. As she saw the pain in Bill's eyes, read the death wishes on his lips, and watched his life ebbing out like water in her kitchen sink, she desperately wished for a way to aid him in finding eternal peace.

But she knew life is a gift from God, no matter the quality. Didn't it appear Bill's life had ended when he had injured his neck in that horrible accident twenty years ago? Hadn't she questioned God in allowing her brother to become a quadriplegic back then? His faith and resilience had been amazing. Since then no one doubted that he had lived a full and productive life.

This time also took them by surprise. For no apparent reason Bill's lungs had filled. A virus attacked. His life was once again teetering on the edge of extinction. Delia's own faith and courage were challenged as never before. It's not easy to commit the life of a loved one into God's hands under such circumstances.

But somewhere during the sixteenth week a miracle transpired. "How long have I been here?" Bill asked one day as if he'd just spent too much time in an airport. He was breathing on his own. He was eating. He was sleeping. As he later wheeled himself out of the hospital, Delia knew God was right. It had not been her brother's time to die.

The ancient Chinese definition of crisis is "an opportunity riding on dangerous winds." Whenever you are faced with a raging storm, remember God is still sovereign. To cut a life off, yours or anyone else's, before the spirit is ready for its eternal destiny would be a horrible injustice. Only God knows the true condition of the soul—and perhaps he'll mend the flesh for another round!

Two Steps Back

- Has there ever been a time when you felt death would be better than life?
- If so, what kept you from acting on those feelings?

Two Steps Forward

- Read Deuteronomy 30:11–20.
- Finish this sentence in your journal: I choose life today by _____

One Step More

Lord, I acknowledge that we are all in Your hands—and You always do what is best if we let You. Help me to let You. Amen.

Rejection

*The LORD is close to the brokenhearted
and saves those who are crushed in spirit.*

Psalm 34:18

I tiptoed through much of my life in fear. God-fearing parents raised me, but the fear of rejection haunted me. I was an extremely sensitive child. I quickly learned that people liked me as long as I didn't make waves, as long as I conformed.

I talked fast so that I wouldn't take up others' time. I pretended I knew more than I actually did so I would appear smart. I kept my humor in check, so my loud laughter wouldn't be offensive. I told white lies to be accepted and seldom refused to do what I was asked.

The fear of rejection was a stronghold in my life. Looking back, I believe God allowed me to experience some difficult times in order for me to know Him—and myself—better.

When life throws you a curve, it may be to straighten you out. After I went through a difficult divorce, God gave me five years of aloneness. He knew I needed the time to get better acquainted with Him—and myself. He gave me certain jobs, certain friends, and certain books that spelled out His unconditional love for me.

When I finally realized that He cherished me *for who I am*, something clicked inside of me. As long as *He* thought I was okay, I didn't need to live my life as a people-pleaser. As long I was a God-pleaser, I didn't have to fear rejection.

Do you feel rejected by someone today? A trusted friend? A spouse? Maybe God? Just remember that He made you the special person you are. Your interests, your talents, your personality, even your body, were all designed so that you could have an extraordinary relationship with Him.

Author and speaker Beth Moore sums it up like this: "God wants to surpass our best dreams, bringing us into a place of obedience that really lasts, into a love that will not fade or fail, and into a genuine freedom that can grow only in the light of His unfailing love."[53]

Two Steps Back

- When have you felt the most rejected?
- When was the last time you experienced rejection?

Two Steps Forward

- Read 1 Samuel 12:19–25.
- Write "God" at the top of a page in your journal and then list all those you count as friends. Whenever you feel rejected, think about those who have accepted you.

One Step More

Lord, thank you for making me the unique person I am. Help me to accept myself because You accept me and love me unconditionally. And help me do the same for others. Amen.

Dealing with Anger

Be angry, and do not sin.

Psalm 4:4

Someone said, "The purpose of anger is to reinforce the expression of hurt." When life wounds us, anger is sometimes the vent we use to release our frustrations. According to scripture, this fiery emotion has its place, but it must be kept in its place.

There are three ways *not* to deal with your inner rage:

Avoidance. Some avoid anger by holding their frustrations in check. They won't talk about their feelings—or even think about them.

Punishment. This is the indirect approach. Some try to get even with others through sulking, holding a grudge, or "the silent treatment."

Attack. This usually involves a direct confrontation, physical or verbal, with accusations flying.

So what's the right thing to do? First, admit you feel angry. Anger in itself is not wrong; it is a valid emotion under certain circumstances. It can, however, be counterproductive. If not handled correctly, it can cripple you and do irreparable damage to others. Unresolved anger will hinder the healing process.

Try to communicate your feelings in a constructive way. Instead of accusing the other party, tell them how the situation has affected you. For instance: "When you left me without giving me child support, it made me feel you didn't care for our children as I thought you did. I can't stand to see them hurting so much."

Ask God to give you the power to forgive. You may have to surrender your cherished resentments over and over. But as you depend on Him—and not yourself—for the strength to let go, you will experience peace.

Once you have dealt with your feelings of hostility through communication and forgiveness, move on. Keep the past in the past. The freedom from anxiety is well worth it.

Two Steps Back

- How do you usually deal with anger? Do you avoid, punish, or attack?
- Are you angry with someone right now?

Two Steps Forward

- Read Ephesians 4:25–32.
- Think through how you might confront this person in a calm and loving manner.

One Step More

God, help me to admit when I'm angry, but keep me in check. Give me the power to forgive and love those who have hurt me. I ask this for Your sake—and mine. Amen.

Break Time

I would hurry to my place of shelter,
far from the tempest and storm.
Psalm 55:8

My daughter, Shanda, called one morning to tell me her two brothers might be stranded on the Big Chief, a stony mountain respected by rock climbers in Canada's British Columbia. Starting their climb the evening before, darkness had hindered their descent. Another climber promised to phone one of their girlfriends, who, in turn, contacted their sister.

I pictured Andrew and Travis, then ages twenty-eight and twenty-seven, roped together on the cleft of a mountain face, exhausted and clinging for their lives. Were they hurt? Had they fallen?

My heart raced as I grabbed my Bible and headed for my "place of shelter," our guest room and my library. This was the one room in our house that I had designated as my spot to meet with God. I desperately needed His comfort now!

He did not disappoint me. When I opened my Bible, I read, "The Lord is my strength... He will make me walk on my high hills" (Habakkuk 3:9, NKJ). I knew that it was His way of telling me that my boys were safe.

I learned later that they had managed to climb to a small ledge on the mountain's face. They had tied themselves to a small, skinny tree and waited the night out. Although they were cold, hungry, and tired, they were safe.

If you are climbing a mountain today, God will provide a shelter for you, a rest spot, so to speak. You may still have lots of climbing ahead of you, but he knows when you need a reprieve from your struggles.

It may not be to your liking (I'm sure my sons would have preferred a hotel with a warm bed and bath!), but it will give you rest to help you keep going. Why not ask God to give you a break in whatever way He sees fit? I'm sure He'd love to do that for you.

Two Steps Back

- Do you need a reprieve from your problems today?
- Do you need to go away for a few days? How about some extra sleep? Can someone take over some of your daily chores?

Two Steps Forward

- Read Psalm 121.
- Make a list in your journal of the possible things you can do to give yourself a break.

One Step More

Lord, You know it's getting pretty dark on this climb. Please provide the rest I need in the shelter of Your choice. Thank You! Amen.

Dealing with Depression

Listen to my cry,
for I am in desperate need.

Psalm 142:6

Several years ago I found myself emotionally needy, and for the first time came face to face with depression. Up until then I had no idea what this "common cold of mental illness" was all about. I just knew something was terribly wrong with me. I couldn't eat or sleep and I was crying in bathrooms a lot.

A gray sadness wrapped itself around me like a warm blanket on a hot summer night. The more I tried to shake it off, the heavier it became. As my condition worsened, I felt more like I was in a deep dark well with slippery sides. I had no strength to climb toward the dim light of normality.

Reading about depression became my first ray of hope. I learned that it could be triggered by stress, a traumatic event, certain medication, hormone irregularities, or drug and alcohol misuse. I recognized many of the symptoms:

- helpless or hopeless
- a loss of interest in normal activities such as hobbies and daily chores
- a lack of interest in others
- a change in sleep habits
- trouble concentrating or making decisions
- feeling tired or weak, or experiencing unexplained pains
- feeling anxious or agitated

- an increase or decrease in appetite and weight
- crying more
- feeling overwhelmed by negative thoughts and emotions
- thoughts and comments about death or suicide
- lack of interest in appearance or hygiene[54]

I should have got professional help, but I did the next best thing. I talked nonstop with a Christian friend, a good listener, with whom I could express my feelings and fears without feeling condemned. I planted some flowers, bought some new clothes, got a new hairdo. I made myself get dressed and go out even if just for a drive. I read the Psalms. I tried to pray. And I kept telling myself depression is not an incurable disease. The book said I would get well. It took time, but I did.

If you identified with the symptoms I mentioned, you too can get the help you need. This *will* pass.

Two Steps Back

- Can you identify with any of the symptoms for depression you just read?
- Do you have any clue as to why you are feeling this way?

Two Steps Forward

- Read Lamentations 3:19–23.
- Tick off the symptoms you identify with. Contact a Christian friend you trust and discuss these feelings.

One Step More

Lord, thank You that You are the Great Physician who heals both mind and body. Please send me the help I need—and give me courage to accept it. Amen.

Heavyweights

Surely God is my help;
the Lord is the one who sustains me.

Psalm 54:4

We have two cherry trees. The backyard one is easy to pick, but the forty-foot-high front-yard one is a challenge. Quite often the birds get the cherries before we do.

Last July, as I worked at my computer in my second-floor home office, I noticed the starlings didn't show up for their annual feast. I watched the luscious fruit on our largest tree turn from green to pink to red to black.

"My mother taught me never to waste food," Allen stated as he climbed a twenty-five-foot extension ladder into the green foliage. He said he would pick the cherries if I stood on the lowest rung to hold it steady. That was one time my extra pounds came in handy!

As I anchored the ladder and watched my ambitious man pick away, I thought about the dreams in life that we fail to accomplish simply because we think they are too difficult or too risky. We forget that there are "heavyweights" who would gladly give us a hand if we only asked.

Look around you. Who do you know is good at intercessory prayer? Who believes in your dreams, in you? Who are the positive thinkers in your life? Do you need a financial backer?

Pray about your dream. Ask God to bring those people to you who will give you support and stability. These "heavyweights" will minimize the risk factor substantially. They will be good company as you pursue what could be a lonely adventure.

We ate the cherries until we had our fill. We gave some away to family and friends. I canned thirty-nine pints and made jam. You too can enjoy the "fruit of your labor." Use your imagination, work hard, and allow God and others to hold you steady.

Two Steps Back

- Who believes in you and your dreams?
- Do you think these "heavyweights" could help you through this crisis?

Two Steps Forward

- Read Psalm 56.
- Make a list of possible "heavyweights." Contact at least one of them and ask for their opinion or assistance.

One Step More

Dear Lord, forgive me if I've doubted the dream You have given me. Help me find those who will hold my ladder while I climb to new heights in You—for Your Glory. Amen.

Your Shepherd

The LORD is my shepherd, I lack nothing.

Psalm 23:1

During Nero's persecution (64 A.D.), the early Christians used symbols as a visible reminder of their faith. These were inscribed on the walls of the catacombs, the marble slabs that sealed the tombs, frescoes, and statues. One of their favorites was that of the Good Shepherd. The shepherd with a lamb around his shoulders represented Christ and the soul that He had saved.

As those oppressed believers gazed at the gentle Shepherd and His injured lamb, they were reminded of the psalmist's words, "The Lord is my shepherd, I shall lack nothing." They also thought of Jesus's parable of the herdsman who had left his flock to find one lost sheep.

Although poor and mistreated, they knew they were far better off than any wealthy pagan. They easily identified with the apostle Paul's words:

"And we know that in all things God works for the good of those who love him... For I am convinced that neither death nor life, neither angels nor demons, neither the present nor the future, nor any powers, neither height nor depth, nor anything else in all creation, will be able to separate us from the love of God that is in Christ Jesus our Lord" (Romans 8:28, 38–39).

As you think about your own problems today, visualize the Good Shepherd lifting you onto His strong shoulders. Remember He found you when you were a lost soul. Do you think He will abandon you now? He wants to hold you in His arms, and carry you to safety. He loves you far more than you can ever imagine.

Two Steps Back

- Think back to the time when you acknowledged Jesus Christ as your Savior and Lord. What difference has that decision made in your life?
- Do you know deep down, no matter how you feel right now, that He has not abandoned you—and He never will?

Two Steps Forward

- Read Isaiah 40:1–11.
- Find or buy a picture that reminds you that Jesus is your Shepherd.

One Step More

Dear Lord Jesus, thank You for finding me when I was far from You. I know You will never abandon me. Help me to trust You with my problems today—and to leave tomorrow's concerns in Your hands. I ask this in Your name. Amen.

A Loving God

He is my loving God and my fortress,
my stronghold and my deliverer,
my shield, in whom I take refuge…

Psalm 144:2

Allen and I have a healthy relationship. We don't tiptoe around each other out of fear. If I spend too much money shopping, I'm not afraid to tell him (well, most of the time!). If he forgets Thursday is Garbage Day, I don't hold it against him. We have learned to give each other room for imperfections and mistakes.

The apostle John knew that unconditional acceptance frees us from the need to qualify or perform in order to experience God's love. In his gospel, he referred to himself five times as "the disciple whom Jesus loved"—although he wasn't perfect. Having witnessed the death and resurrection of his Lord, he later wrote with confidence, "We need have no fear of someone who loves us perfectly" (1 John 4:18).

If you truly believe God loves you, trust your life to Him. Amy Carmichael, a missionary to India for more than fifty years, wrote, "Love God and there will be no room for fear, for to love is to trust and if we trust we do not fear... He has not brought us so far to leave us now."[55]

If you are fearful today, try not to think about what you are dreading. Instead, concentrate on how much God loves you. Remember all the good things He has done for you in the past. Read about His love in the Bible (John 3, 1 John 3–5). Thank

Him for answers to prayer and for His many blessings. And then don't forget: *He has not brought you this far to leave you.*

Two Steps Back

- How would you describe your relationship with God?
- Do you keep commandments out of fear or love?

Two Steps Forward

- Read 1 John 3:16–24.
- Read I Corinthians 13:4-7 and substitute the words "love" or "charity" with "God."

One Step More

Dear Lord, thank You for Your concern for me today. Help me always to remember that You loved me enough to die for me. Forgive me for doubting Your faithfulness. Please accept my love and thankfulness. Amen.

An Anchor

You alone, O Lord, make me dwell in safety.

Psalm 4:8 (NKJ)

Before gas prices went up, Allen and I used to do a lot of fishing in our big old boat. Catching salmon on Canada's west coast was the highlight of our summers. We felt safe sleeping nightly in a certain cove because it was sheltered and perfect for anchorage.

When Allen bought our boat, he discovered he couldn't anchor it just anywhere. He had to study his charts to determine a desirable location because the ocean's floor had to be the right mix of sand and mud in order to "set the hook."

Christians sometime refer to Jesus Christ as their anchor. I prefer, however, to think of Him as the bedrock and hope as the anchor. When the storms of life threaten our peace, He is the solid foundation that holds us steady. Hebrews 6:19 tells us, "We have this hope as an anchor for the soul, firm and secure."

In order to get a "good set," the anchor must be properly embedded. The person who is setting the anchor gives directions to the boat's helmsman to go forward, back, to the right, to the left, until the anchor holds. In the same way, you must be willing to follow the Lord's directions in order to ground your faith. If you insist on calling the shots, you're in trouble.

Allen could usually tell where good anchorage was by reading his charts. Most marine charts indicate the better anchorage spots. In the same way, we establish our faith in Christ by reading the Word of God. One of the best ways to get a grip during a difficult time is to read a Gospel—and remind oneself that He hasn't changed.

It's difficult for one person to set an anchor alone. It's a partnership. And God doesn't expect you to go through this by yourself. Look around. Who has He placed in your path to help you? What about your pastor? A spiritual counselor? A Christian who has survived a similar circumstance? A friend who knows how to pray? Ask God to direct you to the one person who can help you anchor your hopes firmly on Christ.

Two Steps Back

- Do you have a spiritual mentor?
- Are you willing to talk over your fears, frustrations and doubts with a trusted friend or counselor?

Two Steps Forward

- Read Isaiah 25:1–5.
- Contact someone today to help keep you anchored in Christ.

One Step More

Dear Lord, You know my hopes and dreams today. Please help me to anchor them firmly in You. Direct me to those who can help me do this. Amen.

Sleep Strategies

In peace I will lie down and sleep,
for you alone, LORD,
make me dwell in safety.

Psalm 4:8

No one needs to tell you that you need your sleep, especially during a crisis. The required amount of snooze time will vary from one person to another, but your body (especially your mind!) needs its rest in order to function properly.

"Most people are carrying around a tremendous sleep debt, having deprived themselves of adequate rest too many times to remember," stated Dr. James B. Maas, a sleep researcher at Cornell University. *"Too little sleep may also adversely affect your health by putting a damper on your body's natural killer immune cells and reducing your immunity to disease and viral infection."*[56]

Dr. Maas then listed the following "20 Power Sleep Strategies:"

1. Get enough sleep every night.
2. Establish a sleep schedule.
3. Get continuous sleep.
4. Make up for lost sleep.
5. Exercise to stay fit.
6. Keep mentally stimulated during the day.
7. Eat a proper diet.
8. Stop smoking, if you do.
9. Cut back on caffeine.
10. Avoid alcohol near bedtime.

11. Reduce stress.
12. Make your bedroom a haven.
13. Opt for a king-size bed.
14. Don't share your bed with pets.
15. Establish a bedtime ritual.
16. Have pleasurable sex.
17. Don't try too hard to get to sleep.
18. Limit your time in bed.
19. Try relaxation techniques.
20. If you need to, see a sleep specialist.

Number eleven, reducing stress, probably is your biggest challenge right now. That's where faith comes in. The more you place your life and its challenges in the hands of the Lord, the more you will have peace. And the more peace you have, the better you can sleep.

Two Steps Back

- What do you think is hindering you from a good night's sleep?
- What steps have you taken to get more rest?

Two Steps Forward

- Read Psalm 3.
- Reread the list above and make a check beside those things you feel you'd like to try.

One Step More

Dear Lord, You know I need my rest right now. Show me ways to improve my sleep pattern so I can face tomorrow's challenges. Help me to trust You more. Amen.

Small

I am small and despised,
yet I do not forget your precepts.

Psalm 119:141 (NKJ)

Years ago I was involved in helping with monthly Christian services held at a hospital's extended care facility. The Sunday afternoon "congregation" was mostly confined to wheelchairs. Most of them were too weak, blind, or deaf to participate.

I will never forget one of those gatherings. A small group of us had hauled in a box of hymnbooks and musical instruments. We sang. Someone read a scripture and said a few words. Someone else prayed. Just when we thought we were through, Kay, a fellow volunteer, whispered: "I think Eddy should play a song."

Eddy, another volunteer, pulled a harmonica from his pocket, and began to play *Jesus Loves Me*. As the simple melody filled the hospital lounge, I sensed an immediate change in the atmosphere.

Here and there a wobbly voice began to sing:
> *Jesus loves me, this I know,*
> *For the Bible tells me so;*
> *Little ones to him belong,*
> *They are weak, but he is strong.*

Some of the weathered faces were turned upward as they sang. Others shut their eyes. Many wiped tears. Nothing we said or did that afternoon touched them more than that child's song from their distant past.

As I talked with the patients later, I stopped to chat with a woman who was visiting her aging mother. "Mother is ninety-nine," she stated proudly, patting a weathered hand. "She used to be a choir director."

I pictured a young woman standing tall as she confidently conducted Handel's *Messiah.* Now she was a small old woman singing *Jesus Loves Me.* Was God cruel to allow this talented woman to live so long, to suffer the indignities of old age—or was it His way of preparing her for the choruses of heaven?

Jesus said, "Truly I tell you, anyone who will not receive the kingdom of God like a little child will never enter it" (Mark 10:15). Does He allow us to be small—to feel weak, vulnerable, powerless, and out-of-control—so that we can become His children?

Two Steps Back

- Have you given your life to Jesus Christ? Have you asked for His forgiveness?
- Can you say without a doubt that you are His child?

Two Steps Forward

- If you know you are a child of God, write out a testimony: "Jesus loves me, this I know because..."
- If you are not sure, pray the prayer in *One Step More—* and then tell someone.

One Step More

Dear Jesus, I humbly confess to You my sins. Thank you for dying on the cross so I can have a relationship with You and eternal life. I now receive you as my Savior and Lord. Please come into my life and make me a member of Your family. Amen.

Christ's Faith

The Lord is the strength of my life…

Psalm 27:1 (NKJ)

It's easy to talk about faith when life is good or when it's the topic of a sermon or a seminar. Practicing it when your life is turned upside down is quite another thing. When I was diagnosed with cancer, I still believed in God, but like the disciples in the sinking boat, I felt I had to wake Him up.

I know I'm not alone. We think we have to conjure up some magical force called faith. We pray and cry and beg. Or we rely on others to pray and cry and beg for us. We miss the fact that *He* is all we need if He's in the boat!

Inspirational author Eugenia Price (1916–1996) told the story of her own battle with this subject. When tragedy struck close friends of hers, she set aside a certain time each day to pray for them. With fists clenched, jaws set, eyes teary, she worked hard to believe on their behalf. She gave God instructions and visualized His answers. She did this day after day—and nothing happened.

Then one day in total exhaustion, she informed God that she couldn't think of anything else to say. "Good," she seemed to hear him say.

"Then He took over. With simple, swift strokes the Holy Spirit seemed to be drawing a picture that even I could interpret. No words came, but suddenly I *knew* that I had no faith outside of Christ Himself. Suddenly I realized that He Himself is my faith too!"[57]

When Jesus came to dwell in you, He didn't leave His faith in heaven. If He's in your boat, so is His faith. The same faith that gave Him the courage to hang on a cross for your sins is the same faith that can take you through anything.

Eugenia stopped the way she was praying. She began thanking God for His presence and interest in her friends' lives. What a relief! And a few months later the miracle she had hoped for happened.

Two Steps Back

- Have you made a personal commitment to Jesus Christ?
- If so, what keeps you from trusting Him with your concerns today?

Two Steps Forward

- Read Ephesians 2:1–9.
- Write in your journal your own definition of "faith."

One Step More

Dear Lord, forgive me if I underestimate You. Thank You for Your life in me, and the power of Your Spirit. You are all I, and everyone else, need. Amen.

Others

The LORD is good to all;
he has compassion on all he has made.

Psalm 145:9

*"If we obey God it is going to cost other people more than it
cost us... He will look after those who have been pressed into the
consequences of our obedience. We have simply to obey and to
leave all consequences with him."*[58]

This statement by Oswald Chambers never made sense to me
until I had cancer. I didn't believe my illness was God's perfect
will, but I accepted it as His permissive will. I saw my response
as an act of obedience, and it was something not everyone
understood.

I don't like to cause others pain, especially family. As I went
through surgery, chemotherapy, radiation, and hair loss, I knew
they were hurting. I could see it in their eyes, hear it in their
voices. I wanted to help *them.*

It's easy when you're suffering, physically or emotionally, to
become self-absorbed to the point of forgetting that others may
be hurting as well. Acknowledging that your troubles may cause
others discomfort is added stress. I found it helpful to do some
practical things for OTHERS:

Open up. Don't shut others out. Your family and friends
want to help. They *need* to feel they make a difference.

Tell the truth. Honesty will be appreciated. Don't bore them
with details, don't frighten them unnecessarily, but be truthful.

Humor. When our good friend Brien lost both legs to a train
accident, he helped us all cope by joking about his handicap.

"Laughter is the shock absorber of life; it helps us take the blows" (Peggy Noonan).

Explain. Your loved ones may be imagining your situation to be worse than it really is, or they may need to know the hard facts. Talking it out will help all concerned.

Request help. Allow those who love you to help you. It will relieve their sense of helplessness and benefit you. If nothing else, ask them to pray.

Smile. If you want to ease the pain of others watching you suffer, try smiling. It will do you *all* a world of good.

Two Steps Back

- Have you given much thought to how your situation is affecting your family and friends?
- Are you willing to allow them to help you? Have you asked them to pray for you?

Two Steps Forward

- Read Philippians 2:1–11.
- Reach out to someone today. Smile. Let them know how you are doing. Ask them how *they* are doing.

One Step More

Dear Lord, You know I don't like my pain to cause others to hurt. Please make me sensitive to their needs. Bless them for blessing me. Amen.

Making Music

You are my hiding place;
you will protect me from trouble
and surround me with songs of deliverance.

Psalm 32:7

Songs. They can inspire us to "climb every mountain"—or convince us that "nobody knows the trouble I've seen." Even wordless melodies can soothe our spirits, hype us into action, or propel us into depression.

Music is a powerful antidote for misery. Researchers have now discovered that it stimulates the same parts of the brain as food and sex. Using positron emission tomography (PET) scans, they can now actually *see* how music triggers brain systems that make us feel happy.

Several years ago, Allen and I visited an Orthodox church in our area. As visitors, we were allowed to sit on pews positioned against the walls of the sanctuary. The rest of the congregation stood during the entire service. Without any instruments playing, they sang all their songs from the Psalms in beautiful harmony. I will never forget the haunting sound of their voices and the peace I felt as they sang the holy words of praise.

One of the best balms for the soul is the Word of God set to music. The apostle Paul knew this when he told the Christian Ephesians, "Speak to one another with psalms, hymns and songs from the Spirit. Sing and make music from your heart to the Lord, always giving thanks to God the Father for everything, in the name of our Lord Jesus Christ" (Ephesians 5:19–20).

Are you using music, God's gift to you, to lift your spirits? Why not put your feet up and soak in a soothing tune? How about walking or jogging while listening to a fast and happy song?

Try composing a tune to a psalm or remembering the words of an inspirational hymn. Sing in the shower. Hum while you work. Bellow it out while you drive. Find your own "songs of deliverance."

Two Steps Back

- How important is music to you?
- What songs calm you or perk you up?

Two Steps Forward

- Read Psalm 149.
- Try composing a tune to a psalm or remembering the words of an inspirational hymn.

One Step More

Dear God, help me to make music when I don't feel like singing. Direct me to tunes that will get my mind going in a positive direction. Help me to fill my mind with your songs of deliverance. Amen.

Safe

When my father and my mother forsake me,
then the Lord will take care of me.

Psalm 27:10 (NJK)

Nothing captures the hearts of people more than an abandoned child. When the story of a severely depressed mother who abandoned her four-year-old son in a supermarket became national news, the local welfare office was flooded by callers wishing to donate gifts or money.

It has been said that abandonment is the heaviest of all human hurts. Everyone needs to feel wanted and loved. To be forsaken by someone who should love us, such as a parent, is perhaps the deepest emotional wound of all.

A loss in your life can trigger the feeling of being abandoned. Death, divorce, and disease are the biggies. You also can experience rejection through the loss of a job, friend, home, or something else. If the deprivation is severe, you may feel abandoned by God.

The psalmist used the worst possible scenario, the abandonment by a parent, to illustrate God's faithfulness. He had personally experienced the trustworthiness of God through a multitude of tragedies in his own life.

My mother often told me, "If you're ever in trouble, I will come and get you." She was still saying that when she was over eighty! God has made a similar promise to you: "Never will I leave you, never will I forsake you" (Hebrews 13:5).

You may not always feel His presence or see His footprints, but He has not forgotten you. How can He? You are His child and the apple of His eye. He *will* take care of you.

Two Steps Back

- Are you experiencing a loss right now?
- Do you feel abandoned?

Two Steps Forward

- Read Hebrews 13:1–8.
- Make a list of God's promises to you found in this chapter.

One Step More

Dear God, help me to remember You will never leave me no matter what. I need to know You are with me today. Please give me a glimpse of Your presence in whatever way You choose. Amen.

Designed Desperation

I seek you with all my heart;
do not let me stray from your commands.

Psalm 119:10

I know what it's like to feel desperate. There was the time when my children were small, and there was no food in the house to feed them. The occasion when I lost a job that was our only income. And I will never forget how hopeless I felt when my doctor told me I had cancer.

Desperation. It's that feeling of despair when there seems no way out. You have tried everything you can think of to make a situation better, and it just seems to get worse. You don't know whom to talk to or where to turn. As the old saying goes, you are at the end of your rope.

However, hopelessness can be a good thing. It positions you to experience miracles. When you come to the end of *your* resources, God can then take over. He wants to tell you what He told the apostle Paul: *"I am with you; that is all you need. My power shows up best in weak people"* (2 Corinthians 12:9, TLB). I believe He sometimes waits for us to get to a place of desperation. As long as we think we have the answers, we really don't need His help.

This verse as written in *The Message* reads, "I'm single-minded in pursuit of you; don't let me miss the road signs you've posted." God may have allowed you to come to this place of desperation in order to point you in another direction.

So if you are feeling at your wits' end today, take heart. You are in the perfect position for God to give you a special grace.

Miracles do happen. Groceries appeared on my doorstep at the precise moment I needed them. When I lost my job, I was provided with another one. After my cancerous tumor was removed, I had incredible peace and patience through the treatments that followed.

Feeling desperate? It may be just the place God wants you to be.

Two Steps Back

- If you are feeling desperate today, what brought you to this place?
- Are you willing to trust God with your problems?

Two Steps Forward

- Read Deuteronomy 31:6–8.
- Contact someone to pray *with* you today.

One Step More

Lord, I cannot go one more step without You. Please give me a special grace today to seek You with my whole heart—instead of a solution to my problem. Amen.

The Tree Song

Cast your cares on the LORD
and he will sustain you;
he will never let
the righteous be shaken.

Psalm 55:22

I was attending church one Sunday morning during a personal crisis. In his sermon, the pastor told the story about a little boy who was having difficulty getting down from a tree. When his father came to rescue him, the frightened child asked, "Daddy, do I have to let go of everything?"

The man assured his son that he would catch him, but he must first let go of the branches. So, trusting his father's words, the boy jumped into his arms.

The pastor said our heavenly Father wants to free us from our worries and problems, but we must first let go of whatever is holding us back from trusting Him.

That afternoon, as I thought of that little illustration, I wrote these words to music:

I'm up in my tree, just thinking of me
and how to get down.
I hang on to my dreams, hang on to my
schemes, but I'm losing ground.
My Father is calling, but I keep on stalling,
bound by my fears.
He's looking up at me, ready to catch me,
He has been for years.

*It's hard to take chances—there's so many
branches that I'm clinging to.
I just keep on groping, constantly hoping
my dreams will come true.
But my Father who knows me is just trying to
show me how much He cares.
He now has taught me that He will not drop me—
He'll always be there.*

The biggest burden you will ever have is *you.* When you learn to throw yourself—with all your questions and fears—onto the Lord, you will find peace in His everlasting arms. *"Humble yourselves... Cast all your anxiety on him because he cares for you"* (1 Peter 5:6–7).

Two Steps Back

- Has there been a time in your life when you felt totally helpless?
- What did you do then to make things better?

Two Steps Forward

- Read Proverbs 3:1-8.
- Write in your journal: Today I release _____ into God's hands. Picture God holding your burden while you walk away. Promise yourself that you will keep walking!

One Step More

Dear God, I acknowledge today that I cannot solve my problems on my own. I once more give You all that is happening in my life right now. I give You my concerns for today and my fears for the future. Help me not to take them back. Amen.

Hold Tight!

Yet I am always with you;
you hold me by my right hand.

Psalm 73:23

My mother—and her clothes—were my main sources of childhood security. She always made sure we were attached in public places. If her hands were full with groceries or shopping bags, she'd say, "Cathy, hang on to my skirt" or "Cathy, hang on to my sweater."

I will never forget the Woolworth's end-of-the-month sales. My bargain-hunting mother and I often waited with the freezing and frenzied crowds for the doors to open at nine a.m. When an employee with a key appeared, I'd hear, "Okay, Cathy, I'm going to run fast. Just hang on to me." I knew a five-year-old could die from suffocation in such a mad mob, so I obediently grabbed mom's clothes. I was amazed at how far her sweater (and her money) could stretch!

Crossing streets was another matter. Mom would look both ways, grab my hand, and march forth. When it came to *real* danger, she never left it up to me to hang on!

As we journey through life, our heavenly Father asks us to cling to Him—to believe in Him, to trust Him. But sometimes we need to know it's not all up to us. We need to hear, "My child, don't worry. I've got you, and I won't let go!"

During the most difficult times in my life, I heard those words whispered to me in various ways. When I couldn't seem to stretch myself any closer to God, He let me know that He was hanging on to me. What a relief!

My mother didn't hold every child's hand—just her children's. And when I think of my heavenly Father taking me by the hand, I feel special. I know He keeps tabs on everyone, but I like to think of myself as His special child.

When God has us by the hand, we are assured of His presence. We may not always be aware of Him or His dealings, but nevertheless we are safe. And when the psalmist says God holds us by His *right* hand, he wants us to visualize a powerful God who loves us enough to protect us.

Are you feeling detached from God today? When you look at the problems that face you, does He seem far away? Take a few moments now to picture Him holding you with His strong right hand. Do you really think He will let go of you?

Two Steps Back

- Are you feeling far from God today?
- When you consider your problems, does he seem far away?

Two Steps Forward

- Visualize Christ holding your hand. Do you think He will drop you?
- Read Psalm 23.

One Step More

Father, forgive me if I haven't trusted You enough. Help me to remember that You have no intentions of leaving me. Please hang on to me when it's tough for me to hang on to You. Amen.

Father Love

As a father has compassion on his children,
so the LORD has compassion on those who fear him.

Psalm 103:13

When I married Allen, his young adult son came with the package. Chris was out of the nest, but flew back for extended visits—which gave me time to bond with him. Like his dad, he embraces life with opened arms. His enthusiasm is contagious. Whether he's catching a fish, cheering on the Canucks, his favorite hockey team, or landing an account with his firm, he does it with gusto.

When Chris married and became a father, he took his passion for life to a new level.

I have never seen someone more enthusiastic over a child than Chris. To say little Eva brings him joy is an understatement.

On one visit, Chris was attempting to give us some insight into this relationship with his almost-two-year-old daughter. "She loves hockey," he proudly told us. "Whenever there's a game on TV, she and I cuddle together on the couch—and she only cheers for the Canucks! She snuggles really close to me while we eat ice cream and have a great time together."

As I listened to Chris describe his love for his daughter, I thought about my relationship with my Heavenly Father. Does God take as much delight in me as Chris does in little Eva? Do His eyes light up when I enter His presence? Does He love to watch me take steps in a new direction? Does He boast about me to the angels? ("See Cathy down there? I'm so proud of her.

She went through a tough time, but look at her now! I just love that girl!")

The Bible says God IS love. His love is perfect, so it has to surpass the human love we have for our children. Such unconditional love should make us feel valued—and secure. Why should any of us be afraid of the future when our Heavenly Father is watching over us with so much tenderness—and enthusiasm?

Two Steps Back

- Have you ever felt truly loved by someone?
- If so, do you feel God could love you just as much—and more?

Two Steps Forward

- Picture yourself crawling up onto the lap of God. What does it feel like for Him to hold you and enjoy you without wanting anything from you?
- Write in your journal what you think the perfect father would be like. Compare your notes to how you view God.

One Step More

Dear Father, thank You for Your unconditional love. Help me to see Your affection for me in tangible ways. And please show me how to accept Your love—and give You mine in return. Amen.

Dancing in the Rain

Let them praise his name with dancing
and make music to him with timbrel and harp.
For the LORD takes delight in his people;
he crowns the humble with victory.

Psalm 149:3–4

Someone has said, "Life isn't about waiting for the storm to pass. It's about learning to dance in the rain." You will miss a great deal of living if you only focus on a future victory. Abraham received his biggest blessings from God in a hot and barren desert. Moses witnessed his greatest miracles in the wilderness. David wrote his best songs on the battlefield. The apostle Paul penned his finest letters from a jail cell. Jesus Christ accomplished his best work on a cross.

Our trials serve us best when they serve God's purposes. In his book, *Just As I Am*, Billy Graham said, "God created us in His image. He created us and loves us so that we may live in harmony and fellowship with Him. We are not here by chance. God put us here for a purpose, and our lives are never fulfilled and complete until His purpose becomes the foundation and center of our lives."[59]

Thank God for His faithfulness, for the good things He has brought your way. Ask Him what He wants you to learn through this trial. Give Him permission to use you to help someone else. Think about your rainbows instead of your rainfall.

This could be your finest hour. Put on your raincoat, step out into your storm, feel the fresh moisture on your face—and "praise His name with dancing."

Two Steps Back

- Have you responded to God's love for you? Have you accepted Jesus Christ as your personal Savior and Lord?
- Have you glimpsed His plan and purpose through your pain?

Two Steps Forward

- Write a thank-you letter to God in your journal for the good things He has brought your way up to this point.
- Dare to dance again!

One Step More

Dear Father, I may not always see You through the clouds, but I know You are there. Thank You for the plans You have for me, plans to prosper me and not to harm me, plans to give me hope and a future. Amen.

JESUS LOVED ME

Cathy Mogus

Jesus loved me when I was so unlovable,
He died for me before I was born,
He searched for me when I was going my own way,
That's the kind of love you just can't ignore.

He talked to me before I even knew how to pray,
He spent time with me when I wanted only my own way.
He held me in His arms though I struggled to be free,
Before I knew him, He knew all about me.

He looked at me when I couldn't look Him in the eye,
He smiled at me when I did things to make Him cry,
He knew where to find me when I was trying to hide,
Before I wanted Him, He was there by my side.

Make up your own tune!

I'd love to hear from you, so feel free to contact me.

Cathy Mogus
23220 Willett Avenue
Richmond, B.C. V6V 1G1
Canada
acmogus@shaw.ca

Endnotes

[1] Adapted: Cathy Mogus, "God Can Help Us Through The Bad: It's Not the End of the Story," *Esprit,* Summer 1999: 40.

[2] Portions reprinted: Cathy Mogus, "Canned by a Cutback," *Progress,* August/September 1997: 12.

[3] C.S. Lewis, *A Grief Observed* (New York: Harper & Row, 1961).

[4] Isaiah 53.

[5] Amy Carmichael, *Whispers of His Power* (Old Tappan: Fleming H. Revell Company, 1982) p. 86.

[6] Mrs. Charles E. Cowman, *Streams in the Desert* (Grand Rapids: Zondervan Publishing House, 1925).

[7] Michael Kane, "Good Grief: To feel pain is proof you're alive," *The Vancouver Sun,* Sept. 3, 2001: C2.

[8] Robert L. Veninga, *A Gift of Hope: How We Survive Our Tragedies* (New York: Random House, 1985).

[9] Corrie ten Boom, *Each New Day* (Minneapolis: World Wide Publications, 1977) May 11.

[10] Psalm 17:15; 41:12; 55:16; 69:13 (NKJ)

[11] Iris Winston, "Entrepreneur aims for a tailor-made clothes empire," *The Vancouver Sun,* July 7, 2001: D1.

[12] Philippians 4:19 (KJV).

[13] Catherine Marshall, *To Live Again* (New York: McGraw-Hill Book Company, Inc., 1957).

[14] Roger Steer, *J. Hudson Taylor* (Singapore: Overseas Missionary Fellowship [IHQ] Ltd., 1990) p. 159.

[15] Gavin De Becker, *The Gift of Fear: Survival Signals that Protect Us from Violence* (New York: Little Brown and Co., 1997).

[16] Used by permission of the author.

[17] Robert L. Veninga, A *Gift of Hope: How We Survive Our Tragedies* (New York: Random House, Inc., 1985).

[18] Eugene H. Peterson, *The Message: Psalms* (Colorado Springs: Navpress.1994) Psalm 63:6.

[19] Dwight Carlson, M.D. and Susan Carlson Wood, *When Life Isn't Fair (*Eugene: Harvest House Publishers, 1989) p. 163.

[20] Amy Carmichael, *Whispers of His Power* (Old Tappan: Fleming H. Revell Company, 1982) p. 216.

[21] Catherine Marshall, *To Live Again* (New York: McGraw-Hill Book Company, Inc., 1957).

[22] David B. Posen, M.D., "5 Ways to Conquer Worry," *Reader's Digest*, October 1999: 67.

[23] Larry King, *Powerful Prayers* (Los Angeles: Renaissance Books, 1998) pp. 101,102.

[24] Adapted: Cathy Mogus, "Are You Stuck?" *Purpose*, July 13, 2008: 6.

[25] Eric J. Cassell, M.D., *The Healer's Art: A New Approach to the Doctor-Patient Relationship* (New York: Harper & Row, Inc., 1976), p. 44.

[26] Dwight Carlson and Susan Carlson Wood, *When Life Isn't Fair* (Eugene: Harvest House Publishers, 1989) p. 137.

[27] Lonnie Dupre, *Greenland Expedition: Where Ice is Born* (Minnetonka: NorthWord Press, 2000).

[28] Rick Warren, *The Purpose Driven Life* (Grand Rapids: Zondervan, 2002) pp. 107, 111.

[29] Mildred Stamm, *Meditation Moments* (Grand Rapids: Zondervan Publishing House, 1967) Sept. 11.

[30] John Walsh with Susan Schindehette, *Tears of Rage: From Grieving Father to Crusader for Justice: The Untold Story of the Adam Walsh Case* (New York: Simon & Schuster Inc., 1997).

[31] Lance Armstrong and Sally Jenkins, *It's Not About the Bike— My Journey Back to Life* (New York: G.P. Putnam's Sons, 2000) p. 62.

[32] Robert L. Veninga, *A Gift of Hope: How We Survive Our Tragedies* (New York: Random House, Inc., 1985) p. 180.

[33] Doug Anakin, "Olympian's Secret to Success," *Freedom 55 Financial* brochure, London Life Insurance Co., 2001.

[34] Reprinted by written permission of the author.

[35] Oswald Chambers, *My Utmost for His Highest* (New York: Dodd, Mead & Company, 1935) p. 310.

[36] *The Vancouver Sun,* September 27, 2000.

[37] Dwight Carlson and Susan Carlson Wood, *When Life Isn't*

Fair—Why We Suffer and How God Heals (Eugene: Harvest House Publishers, 1989) p. 82.

[38] Viktor Frankl, *Man's Search for Meaning* (New York: Washington Square Press, 1959) p.121.

[39] Oswald Chambers, *My Utmost for His Highest* (New York: Dodd, Mead & Company, 1935) p. 310.

[40] Oswald Chambers, *My Utmost for His Highest*, Updated Edition (Grand Rapids: Discovery House Publishers, 1995) Feb. 13.

[41] Isobel Kuhn, *Green Leaf in Drought-Time* (Chicago: Moody Press, 1957) p. 14.

[42] Oswald Chambers, *My Utmost for His Highest* (New York: Dodd, Mead & Company, 1935) August 10.

[43] Portions reprinted: Cathy Karr, "A Light for My Path," *Pentecostal Testimony*, 1985: 34.

[44] Robert L. Veninga, *A Gift of Hope: How We Survive Our Tragedies* (New York: Random House, Inc., 1985) p. 75.

[45] Quoted in Robert L. Veninga, *A Gift of Hope: How We Survive Our Tragedies* (New York: Random House, Inc., 1985) p. 76.

[46] Oswald Chambers, *My Utmost for His Highest* (New York: Dodd, Mead & Company, Inc., 1935) Nov. 20.

[47] Dr. James Dobson, *Focus on the Family Bulletin* (Carol Stream: Tyndale House Publishers, Inc., 1999).

[48] Oswald Chambers, *My Utmost for His Highest* (New York: Dodd, Mead & Company, 1935) Aug. 23.

[49] Tim Hansel, *You Gotta Keep Dancin'* (Elgin: David C. Cook Publishing Company, 1985) p. 76.

[50] Jeremiah 33:3 (KJV).

[51] Amy Carmichael, *Whispers of His Power* (Old Tappan: Fleming H. Revell Company, 1982) p. 31.

[52] Dr. Seuss, *Oh, the Places You'll Go!* (New York: Dr. Seuss Enterprises, L.P., Random House, Inc., 1990).

[53] Beth Moore, *Breaking Free Day by Day: A Year of Walking in Liberty* (Nashville: B & H Publishing Group, 2007) Introduction.

[54] Partially quoted from *Contact* (Great-West Life Newsletter) Volume 8, Issue 2.

[55] Amy Carmichael, *Whispers of His Power* (Old Tappan: Fleming H. Revell Company, 1982).

[56] James B. Mass, Ph. D., "The Healing Power of Sleep," *Family Circle,* Sept. 15, 1998: 63.

[57] Eugenia Price, *Early Will I Seek Thee* (New York: The Dial Press, 1956, 1983) p. 36.

[58] Oswald Chambers, *My Utmost for His Highest* (New York: Dodd, Mead & Company, 1935), Jan. 11.

[59] Billy Graham, *Just As I Am* (San Francisco: HarperCollins Worldwide, 1997) p. 727.

Printed in Great Britain
by Amazon

41504424R00159